YANKEE MAGAZINE'S

The
New England
We Love

OUR
FAVORITE PLACES

FROM
YANKEE'S EDITORS

Some of the material in this book previously appeared, before revision, in *The Yankee Traveler* newsletter, *Yankee Magazine's Travel Guide to New England*, and *Yankee* Magazine.

Text design by Karen Savary
Cover photo by Kindra Clineff

Library of Congress Cataloging-in-Publication Data is available.

ISBN 0-7627-0441-1
Co-published by Yankee Publishing Inc. and The Globe Pequot Press. Distributed to the trade by The Globe Pequot Press. Produced by Yankee Publishing Inc.

Printed in Canada.

First Edition
2 4 6 8 10 9 7 5 3 1 softcover

Contents

Vermont

New Hampshire

Massachusetts

Preface

THE FIRST TIME I MET JUDSON HALE SR., EDITOR OF *Yankee* Magazine, was in 1976. He was appearing as a guest on a public-television news program, and I was one of his questioners. I decided to catch him off guard. "Mr. Hale," I said belligerently, "doesn't *Yankee* promote a mythical view of New England?"

"Yes," he said. "But myths are important."

So much for ambush journalism. He was in control of the interview from that point on. But I learned a couple of important lessons. One is that the best way to disarm a hostile questioner is to agree with him. The second is that a myth is not the same thing as a lie. A myth represents something we hope and wish to be true — something we aspire to, even if the reality falls short of our aspirations.

I came to work for *Yankee* Magazine just a few months later, and in the 22 years since, I've frequently been asked the same question, in different words, by other aggressive reporters. "Isn't New England pretty much the same as everywhere else these days?" they ask, hoping to put me on the defensive.

"Yes," I say, using Jud-jitsu. "If you stay on the interstates and inside the shopping malls. The other New England — the New England of small towns, and country stores, and white-clapboarded Colonial houses huddled around a green — does exist. But you have to get out of the malls and off the interstate to find it."

This message is often greeted with a skeptical oh-sure look, but it's true. I know the postcard towns exist because I live in one of them. Dublin, New Hampshire, has 1,500 residents, two general stores, one blinking yellow traffic light, a deep, cold, clean lake (that at one time had its own species of trout), a prep school, a petting farm, and about one-third of the land of the world's most frequently climbed mountain, Mount Monadnock. We have several churches and white-clapboarded houses aplenty, but no picturesque town green — just a little grassy oval in the middle of Route 101 with a flagpole, a green historic plaque describing us (incorrectly) as the highest town in New Hampshire, and a big rock.

That's not unusual — the absence of the green, I mean. Most postcard towns are short one or two elements of the dream machinery. Or they have things that don't fit in the postcard — Dublin has two facilities for people trying to kick drug and alcohol habits, for example. Some people might find that jarring. I like it. I don't want to live in Grover's Corners. We don't sit around the country stores whittlin', nobody calls me "Editor Clark," and I haven't met a single man named Eben. People here are like people everywhere — we gripe about taxes, rent videos, get divorced, worry about our weight, argue about politics, and say dumb things that we later regret.

But every now and then I lift my head and see a black-and-white pony grazing under a yellow maple tree on a green field in front of a red barn. Or the sun comes out after an ice storm, turning the winter woods into the world's biggest chandelier. Or I join the whole town marching up the hill to the cemetery on Memorial Day, and the scent of the purple lilacs along the road threatens to stop us in our tracks.

And I think: The New England of our hopes and dreams does exist. I'm lucky enough to live and work and raise my family here.

That's what *Yankee* Magazine — and this book, *The New England We Love* — is for. We tell you where to find the mythical New England — the postcard towns like Dublin or our next-door neighbor, Hancock, New Hampshire; the perfect college settings, like Williamstown, Massachusetts; the cool, clean mountain lakes of Vermont's Northeast Kingdom; the astonishing jumble of antiques shops in Rhode Island's East Bay; the unspoiled natural wonders of Connecticut's tidelands; and the Maine harbors shrouded with fog as the lobster boats go out at sunrise. For those of you who want to visit our mythical towns, we have included a bonus chapter at the end of the book that is a sampler of some of our favorites. We share with you the real voices and experiences of our longtime friends, editors, and writers who have written here about the New England we love.

We invite you to see for yourself.

– TIM CLARK
Managing Editor, *Yankee* Magazine

Acknowledgments

I WOULD LIKE TO THANK MY COLLEAGUES IN THE Travel Group: Mel Allen, editorial director, whose creativity all of us at Yankee Publishing have come to rely on over the years. He gave us the concept for this book, saying at one editorial meeting last year, "Let's just write about the places we love the most." Carol Connare, associate editor, whose good writing, editorial skills, enthusiasm, and energy we have enjoyed and depended on for more than two years. Erica Bollerud, editorial assistant, is the newest member of our team. Erica worked for us as an intern one summer, and we quickly snagged her upon her graduation from Williams College. Her very first story (a good-bye to Williams) appears here. Thanks to Jean Camden for keeping the office running smoothly. All of us in the Allison House appreciate her support and her hard work.

This is the second travel book we have asked Karen Savary to design. We were so pleased with the first, *Yankee Magazine's Great Weekend Getaways in New England*, that we knew we could count on Karen's good eye for this book, too. A big thanks goes to Jamie Trowbridge, publishing director, for his consistent encouragement, humor, and leadership and for being a darned good book editor. Tim Clark, managing editor of *Yankee* Magazine, kindly wrote the preface for us. When talking about the book in its early stages, he remarked that the classic New England village symbolized what we love about this region; we can always count on Tim for the perfect metaphor. I would like to thank Janice Brand, my predecessor. Some of the stories here, including her wonderful piece on the prettiest towns, are the result of her keen editorial work.

Special thanks to our Production Department: Paul Belliveau, production director, whose job description should read "crisis management," which everyone at Yankee Publishing knows he does with unrivaled aplomb. Dave Ziarnowski, production manager, whose steady hand guides his staff through some of the most amazing deadlines. Lucille Rines, Rachel Kipka, and Brian Jenkins (especially for the wonderful maps he produced) for their speed, emotional equanimity, and technical skills in producing page, after page, after page, and getting them all right! Thanks to Christine Halvorson and Stephanie McCusker for dogged fact checking. We are grateful to copy editors Lida Stinchfield and Lynn Sloneker for their attention to the details that make this book eminently readable and useful.

I extend a huge thanks to the writers and editors whose work we have included here. *Yankee* Magazine and *Yankee Magazine's Travel Guide to New England* could not enjoy the success we have without their bright ideas and deft writing. Judson D. Hale Sr., longtime editor of *Yankee* and *The Old Farmer's Almanac*, deserves an expression of gratitude. Jud Hale personifies "The New England We Love." Born in Boston, raised in the north woods of Maine, an Ivy Leaguer whose favorite pastime is taking a spin in his powerboat, Jud embodies more aspects of the New England character than anyone we know.

– POLLY BANNISTER
Managing Editor, *Yankee* Travel Group

Introduction

I MUST CONFESS THAT I AM NOT A NATIVE NEW Englander. I was raised among the cornfields of Ohio. But from the moment I read the book *Johnny Tremain* by Esther Forbes at ten, I was hooked on New England. Five minutes after receiving my college degree in Indiana, I headed east. I've lived in four of the six New England states, including long stays on islands in Rhode Island and Maine. When I settled, it was to work in New Hampshire at *Yankee* Magazine. At the time I considered myself fortunate to find a job where one of the responsibilities was to explore New England. Now, nearly 20 years later, I still think I'm lucky. Over the years of editorial work I have had the pleasure of visiting many, many places in the region. When I am on the road, I always think the same thing: that I am convinced I will live in New England for the rest of my life and that for those folks who can't do the same, they should visit often. New England is a great travel destination, where even first-time visitors feel as though they're coming home.

Our compact six-state area offers tremendous variety — mountains for hiking and skiing, miles of coastline, pic-

turesque Colonial villages (just like I imagined when reading
Johnny Tremain), farmland dotted with Holsteins, historic
cities alive with culture, and deep wilderness. And best of all,
an energetic traveler can see all this inside one day. Each
time I set out on a trip in New England, I know I will learn
something new and see something beautiful. That is what
this book is all about. We have selected stories that will tell
you interesting facts, such as where the nation's oldest continuously operating agricultural fair is or the world's most
climbed mountain. Stories that will take you to the most
beautiful places we know, like a Vermont field where hundreds of snow geese migrate annually or Maine's Acadia National Park on a sparkling winter morning. In more than 60
years of writing about New England, the editors of *Yankee*
conclude that you will not find a more interesting, lovely,
historic, and fun place to visit. And within these pages we
share some of our first choices.

Here is how to use this book to make the most of your
travels: Each state has specially selected stories highlight-
ing favorite destinations that we think truly characterize
that state. For example, Newport, Rhode Island, is considered to be the most beautiful port in the Ocean State. And
in Boston, our nation's birthplace, we celebrate Patriots
Day with an itinerary guaranteed to inspire loyalty and
keep you hopping. Each story is followed by a map and editors' picks for the area. Here we have hand-picked places
we know you'll find top-notch and have provided reviews
and the essentials (addresses, phone numbers, hours, and
prices) for over 350 inns, B&Bs, restaurants, museums, and
other attractions.

With each restaurant we note the average price of an
entrée with the following code:

$ — most entrées under $10
$$ — most entrées $10-$16
$$$ — most entrées $17-$23
$$$$ — over $23

As in our earlier book of driving tours, entitled *Yankee Magazine's Great Weekend Getaways in New England*, we include our popular feature "What the Locals Know." These are insiders' tips from town clerks, shopkeepers, librarians, and other local residents. In the process of editing this book and stories for *Yankee* Magazine and *Yankee Magazine's Travel Guide to New England*, we have asked these locals for their favorite views, walks, shopping bargains, bakeries, and more. Their secrets are highlighted wherever you see this symbol to the left.

As a bonus we have provided an extra chapter called "Our Towns — A Sampler of New England's Prettiest." This is a roundup of some of our all-time favorites — postcard-perfect villages that fuel our most romantic vision of the region. Though the entire book is guaranteed to inspire, we consider this last chapter a grand finale tour of our most classic images: fine Colonial homes with bright white clapboards and black shutters, town greens lined with maple trees in full fall color, bandstands decorated with American flags. We invite you to share these classics and more in *The New England We Love*.

– POLLY BANNISTER
Managing Editor, *Yankee* Travel Group

Maine

Goat Island Light, Kennebunkport *(photo by Robert Dennis, courtesy Kennebunk/Kennebunkport Chamber of Commerce)*

Ogunquit, Half Off

Off-Season in One of Southern Maine's Most Popular Towns

THE OCEAN IS AVAILABLE ALL YEAR ROUND — IT never closes for renovation, it has no seasonal hours. Yet after Labor Day, most New England tourists are pressing leaves and puffing up overpopulated mountain paths.

We feel differently, so we headed to Ogunquit, a small town in southern Maine with less than 1,000 residents year-round (three or four times that in summer). We stayed at the Dunes, a compound of piney, briny cabins scattered along a tidal flat behind a busy motel complex off Route 1. When the tide is out, the Ogunquit River stretches dryly to sand dunes and past them to the ocean itself.

We bunked in Cottage #18, a woody dollhouse with one great room that held a fireplace, two sofa beds, and a nautical mirror in the shape of a sailor's wheel. There was an instruction sheet in the kitchen for guests: nothing about garbage disposals or emergency exits, but detailed instructions on using the rowboats "from 2½ hours before high tide to 2½ hours after high tide."

Petunias drooped from window boxes, as if the summer had worn them out, and a family of chipmunks sat on the roof, chewing industriously as if their lives depended on it. We strolled past sandpipers sitting on a fleet of beached, purposeless-looking rowboats. A footbridge on the opposite shore led through the dunes to the edge of the sea. An autumn ocean is no place for sunsuits and beach blankets. It is gray, rough, and intelligently untouched by human toes.

We turned onto the Marginal Way, a path of beach roses and berry bushes above the ocean cliffs. "Marginal" is a misnomer, for the mile-long way has been central to Ogunquit's serenity since it was built in 1925 by the Honorable Josiah Clark of York, Maine. A large woman in an "I love the Grand Ole Opry" sweatshirt passed us.

"Hill coming," she said, energetically pumping her arms and wasting no breath on pronouns. "Gotta put it in second gear!"

As we sat on one of the many scattered benches, we wondered about bench etiquette in the uncrowded fall: Do they have a maximum occupant capacity, like elevators? Then the Opry lover reappeared and lowered herself beside us. She had a man in tow; he wore pants with a patchwork-quilt design and a tam-o'-shanter cap. They noticed a cormorant on the rocks below us.

"That bird can't swim," she said. It bobbed wildly, then suddenly dived and disappeared.

"He's chowing down under there. He's fine. Let's keep going," her companion said.

"I'm not leaving until I see him again."

"But we have to be back by two."

"I'm staying."

"Well," said the man, "then I got plenty of time, too."

She looked at him affectionately. "You cave in like a paper bag," she said, and they sat with shoulders touching.

The Marginal Way was dotted with a series of green trash barrels, each painted with a single word. Forgiveness. Generosity. Faithfulness. Sincerity. Honesty. Sympathy. The last barrel repeated the quality of the first. We thought we understood why. There can never be enough space to hold Forgiveness.

In Perkins Cove, a cul-de-sac of galleries and restaurants at the end of the Marginal Way, we sat over bowls of chowder and over the harbor boats. Our relaxed waiter served us salads and, in no particular hurry, followed our gaze.

Ogunquit Beach offers three miles of sand and surf to beach lovers throughout the year. (photo by Nancy G. Horton, courtesy Ogunquit Chamber of Commerce)

"Peaceful," he said, as if this were his first chance to realize it.

"What do you do here in the fall?"

"Replenish," he said. "Fresh pepper?"

Autumn is the season of resolution as well as replenishment, and the couple next to us were taking an accounting over their meals.

"I've got to work more," the woman said.

"I've got to work less," the man said.

Ogunquit has been an art colony since 1873, and low one-room galleries stand shoulder to shoulder with their doors open in Perkins Cove. The proprietor of George Carpenter Gallery sat on his stoop in a sailing cap. A black spaniel sat in his lap. Both were eating french fries.

We stopped in at Scully Gallery, a one-woman exhibit at the end of the dock, past the harbormaster's office, the empty lobster-boat fishing space, and the posted warning to striped-bass fishermen about proper harvest methods and creel limits. The gallery walls were covered with calligraphy — the words of like-minded thinkers like John Lennon and the Talmud — and familiar watercolor scenes: The same views framed outside by windows were framed inside by wood. The owner wore a bulky sweater. "Don't have any heat," she said. "Closing soon."

There were jewelry stores with seashell bracelets and clothing stores with Ogunquit memorabilia. Everything was on sale. It was as if, with the end of summer, the town was going out of business and offering itself half off.

In Perkins Cove Candies — a narrow, ivy-covered house — we found the best of nostalgia: urns of licorice wheels, gummy bears, and spice drops; buckets of candy-filled pinwheels; baskets of caramel corn and pulled taffy; boxes of fudge. Beyond it, a wall that was all windows looked out over rock and wave, and a colony of gulls looked in with unconcealed envy.

As the afternoon ended, we walked across the Perkins Cove drawbridge — the only pedestrian drawbridge in

America — and a prime location for the autumn sunset. It bounced lightly as we crossed. Someone had nailed a row of birdhouses onto the wooden pilings, an avian condo community, empty now, but no doubt with long waiting lists by Memorial Day.

It was nippy, even by our standards, and we took the trolley back to the Dunes. "Tulip" had brass poles and stenciled windows. We were her only riders. The gray-haired

Where to Find the Best Maine Souvenir

Just a little north of Ogunquit — in Wells — you'll find the largest collection of lighthouse gifts anywhere. Kathy Finnegan and Tim Harrison run Lighthouse Depot Gifts, where they stock over 7,000 lighthouse items ranging from 99¢ trinkets to five-foot, fully operational "lawn lighthouses" for about $700. There are lighthouses on driftwood, postcards, puzzles, beer steins, cookie cutters, ornaments, trivets, and just about anything else you can think of, plus the most complete collection of lighthouse videos and books anywhere. You can subscribe to their monthly magazine, *Lighthouse Digest,* for $24 (one-year subscription) or $42 (two years). A mail-order catalog is available free.

Lighthouse Depot Gifts, 2190 Post Rd., Rte. 1 North, P.O. Box 427, Wells, ME 04090-0427. Open year-round, except major holidays; high season 9-8, Sunday 10-5; off-season hours vary a bit (call ahead). 800-758-1444, 207-646-0515.

Tim Harrison, Lighthouse Depot. (photo by George Riley)

driver blew her nose and turned around. "Heading anywhere special, dears?" she asked. "This time of year, you treasure every customer."

We thought about the unspoken tension a summer town surely feels. It exists by the grace of tourists; those who live in it depend on those who visit and leave. Yet even these towns must look forward to the end of summer. Autumn is their seventh day, when they rest at last.

We returned to #18 Dunes, our simple woody address, like travelers crossing between civilizations. The frost had arrived. We built a fire and poured glasses of wine. We stretched our feet out on #18's braided rugs and thought that, at this moment, in this world, only four things mattered.

Fire. Ocean. Dunes. Autumn.

– Elissa Ely

Editors' Picks for Ogunquit

General Information

Ogunquit Chamber of Commerce, Rte. 1 South, P.O. Box 2289, Ogunquit, ME 03907. 207-646-2939. (www.ogunquit.org)

Tourist Information Bureau, Rte. 1 South, Ogunquit, ME 03907. 207-646-5533.

Southern Maine Coast Information Line, 800-639-2442.

Where to Stay

Ogunquit is second only to Bar Harbor as far as Maine's greatest number of summer guests. There are about 4,000 rooms available in the Ogunquit area, and here are just a few of our favorites.

The Dunes on the Waterfront, Rte. 1, P.O. Box 917, Ogunquit, ME 03907. 207-646-2612. This property is set off the road on 12 acres that front the Ogunquit River, with access to Ogunquit Beach. Owned and operated by the Perkins family for over 60 years. Open May-October. Coffee and tea service included. Cottages: $80-$145, suites $80-$125, motel rooms $65-$135. (www.dunesmotel.com)

The Beachmere Inn, 12 Beachmere Place, P.O. Box 2340, Ogunquit, ME 03907. 800-336-3983, 207-646-2021. Located on the Marginal Way, this property has the same traditional feel as the Dunes and is also owned and operated by third-generation Ogunquit residents. A hotel complex with 54 rooms. Open March-December. Continental breakfast included. $65-$180. (www.beachmereinn.com)

The Sparhawk, 41 Shore Rd., P.O. Box 936, Ogunquit, ME 03907. 207-646-5562. The only AAA four-diamond property in town, this snazzy luxury motel offers 55 oceanfront units, plus 27 ocean-view suites and three apartments. Pool, shuffleboard, tennis, and croquet. Open mid-April to October. Continental breakfast included. $80-$170.

Juniper Hill Inn, 196 Rte. 1, P.O. Box 2190, Ogunquit, ME 03907. 800-646-4544, 207-646-4501. There are 100 rooms in this complex of buildings located right on the water. Luxurious rooms, indoor pool, heated outdoor pool, sauna, and gardens. Open year-round. $43-$154. (www.ogunquit.com)

Where to Eat

Arrows, Berwick Rd. (1.8 miles from Rte. 1 downtown), Ogunquit. 207-361-1100. We have never met anyone who didn't have a great meal here. Located in a 1700s farmhouse, this restaurant features nouvelle cuisine with fresh, local ingredients. Open late April-late November, always closed Monday. Open July and August Tuesday-Sunday for dinner; in May and after Columbus Day open for dinner Friday, Saturday, and Sunday. Reservations recommended. $$$$.

98 Provence, 104 Shore Rd., Ogunquit. 207-646-9898. Like Arrows, this restaurant consistently receives rave reviews. Casual and intimate, decorated with Provençale linens and tableware, it offers the only French cuisine in town. Seasonal menu with such delicious entrées as farm-raised Maine venison served with wild berry sauce and a very popular duck dish served with black truffle and foie gras. Open April to mid-December daily, except Tuesday, for dinner. $$$.

Jackie's Too, Perkins Cove, Ogunquit. 207-646-4444. A perennial favorite with families, here you will find everything from lobster rolls to hamburgers, spaghetti, and great seafood. Casual dining with a beautiful ocean view. Open year-round daily; in summer 11-10; off-season weekdays for lunch only; off-season weekends 11-9. $$.

Strolling the Kennebunks

Fine Architecture Along the South Coast

JUNE IS A GLORIOUS MONTH TO BE IN KENNEBUNK and neighboring Kennebunkport. Those of us who live here are filling our doorstep pots with impatiens or geraniums or trailing lobelia. Pink beauty bush and cascading bridal wreath decorate our dooryards, where cardinals startle us with their thrilling song. Nature is as intent as we are on making our villages beautiful.

People visit the Kennebunks because of George Bush, our beaches, or shopping, I suppose. But this June ritual of beautifying our homes highlights one of the best reasons for coming here — our rich architectural heritage. The two villages, both of which have historic districts on the National Register, are filled with fine examples from all the major American periods. Kennebunk's Brick Store Museum, itself an outstanding Federal commercial building, offers an illustrated walking tour for those with a serious interest in architecture. But just to look around here is satisfying enough.

After 30 years in Kennebunk I still take pleasure from the view at the turn from Main Street to Summer Street. I look one way to the museum and the other to the 1772 First Parish Church, where a Paul Revere bell hangs in the balustraded steeple. Always, passing the dignified Summer Street houses built by two generations of moneyed maritime families, I am caught in reverie by their grandeur and history. As a local historian, I know in which houses women waited for their seafarers. One woman, in dying delirium, called for all the lamps to be lit as a beacon for her long-lost son.

A five-minute drive away is Kennebunkport's Dock Square, where another walking tour is available at Kennebunk Book Port. Tours are available at the Kennebunkport Historical Society's House, Nott House. According to the

Former president Bush's summer house is located on Walker's Point, a private 11-acre peninsula. *(photo by Robert Dennis, courtesy Ogunquit Chamber of Commerce)*

A Real Working Port

Joyce Butler, who has lived in Kennebunk for over 30 years, says, "Locals know that you haven't really visited Kennebunkport until you've been to the pier at Cape Porpoise." She adds, "Here is a real working port, where you'll see the fishermen in their big rubber boots and smell the bait. There's an interesting marker that commemorates a rare Maine Revolutionary battle, and you can take in a lovely view of the Goat Island Lighthouse." It is this view that Champlain called "Le Port aux Isles," or island harbor, when he spotted it in 1605. Now that the Conservation Trust has taken over much of this area, including the scattered islands, this view will be forever preserved.

guide, a German traveler in 1819 marveled at the village houses "built very delicately of wood . . . covered with boards lying on each other like scales on a fish." Interesting stuff, but you don't need a guide to appreciate the workmanship here. When I visit the Graves Memorial Public Library, the needs of children no longer take me to the second floor; yet now and again, I climb the stairs to see the 1930 fairy-tale murals that delighted my toddlers.

I like to stroll along the Cape Arundel promontory at the end of a June day. I leave my car near St. Ann's Church and follow the road on foot past banked *Rosa rugosa*, looking to the ocean for lazy sailboats not yet ready to run to harbor. The simple song of someone's wind chime seems incongruous with the fanciful oversized "cottages" I pass along the way. I end my outward walk at Walker's Point, where George and Barbara Bush entertained world leaders in their 1903 summer house, giving them the American experience of being at home — in the Kennebunks.

— Joyce Butler

Editors' Picks for the Kennebunks

General Information

Kennebunk/Kennebunkport Chamber of Commerce, Western Ave. (at the junction of rtes. 9 and 35 in the lower village of Kennebunk), P.O. Box 740, Kennebunk, ME 04043. 800-982-4421, 207-967-0857. (www.kkcc.maine.org)

Where to Stay

Captain Lord Mansion, (corner of Pleasant and Green sts.), P.O. Box 800, Kennebunkport, ME 04046. 800-522-3141, 207-967-3141. A big, beautiful sea captain's house built in 1812, with high ceilings, huge fireplaces, and a four-story elliptical staircase that leads to an octagonal cupola. There are 16 large, luxurious rooms, most with gas fireplaces (they use about 7,000 Duraflame logs a year), four-poster beds, and other antiques everywhere. Breakfast is served family style at two long farm tables in a country kitchen. Open year-round. Breakfast included. $125-$349. (www.captainlord.com)

Captain Fairfield Inn, 8 Pleasant St., P.O. Box 1308, Kennebunkport, ME 04046. 800-322-1928, 207-967-4454. A Federal-style mansion built a year later than neighbor Captain Lord Mansion. Fairfield's portrait, which was retrieved from a shipwreck and miraculously returned to his family after his death, hangs in the Brick Store Museum. The nine large, graciously appointed rooms are open year-round. Breakfast and afternoon tea included. $89-$225. (www.captain-fairfield.com)

The Maine Stay Inn & Cottages, 34 Main St., P.O. Box 500A, Kennebunkport, ME 04046. 800-950-2117, 207-967-2117. Located in a quiet residential area designated a Historic Preservation District. The main house, built in 1860, with its deep wraparound porch and cupola, houses six rooms, including two suites. Guests seeking more privacy can stay in one of 11 spacious cottage rooms, where they have the option of having a breakfast basket delivered to their door. Open year-round. Full breakfast included. $85-$215. (www.mainestayinn.com)

1802 House, 15 Locke St., P.O. Box 646-A, Kennebunkport, ME 04046. 800-932-5632, 207-967-5632. In the original part of the house, which has been added onto over the years, you'll find six guest rooms, each offering a fireplace or whirlpool (or both if you're looking for a really sensuous stay). Open year-round. Breakfast included. $119-$299. (www.1802inn.com)

Where to Eat

Arundel Wharf Restaurant, Ocean Ave., Kennebunkport. 207-967-3444. You'll feel surrounded by water — and the view — while indulging in some casual dining on the large outdoor deck above the Kennebunkport River or seated in the mahogany-accented dining room decorated with brass and model ships. Just try to decide between the eight featured Maine lobster entrées. Open mid-April to October; open high season Sunday-Thursday 11:30-9:30, Friday and Saturday 11:30-10; off-season hours vary (call ahead). Reservations recommended for dinner. $$-$$$$.

Kennebunkport Inn, One Dock Sq., Kennebunkport. 207-967-2621. Located in a sea captain's 1899 Victorian home in the heart of Kennebunkport. Have an intimate dining expe-

rience near the fireplace in the captain's parlor, or eat al
fresco at the sidewalk café during the summer. The menu
specializes in native seafoods and classic sauces. Features a
piano bar weekends in May, nightly June-October. Open
mid-May to October daily for breakfast, lunch, and dinner.
Reservations recommended. $$$-$$$$.

Salt Marsh Tavern, 46 Western Ave., Kennebunkport. 207-
967-4500. Perched on the tidal marsh above Kennebunk
Beach, this restaurant offers unspoiled views as well as eclec-
tic New England cuisine. The seasonal menu is served on
white linen in a candle-lit barn furnished with antiques, sur-
rounded by three acres of extensively landscaped gardens.
Features an evening piano bar. Open (nearly) year-round
daily for dinner. Reservations recommended. $$$-$$$$.

White Barn Inn, 37 Beach St., Kennebunkport. 207-967-
2321. The charming contrast between the rusticity of its set-
ting in a Civil War-era farmhouse and its formal elegance as
Maine's only five-diamond restaurant makes this the place to
go when you have something big to celebrate. Features
American regional cuisine, with Maine specialties such as
steamed lobster on a bed of homemade fettuccine with
carrot-ginger snow peas. Open (nearly) year-round daily for
dinner. Reservations required. Fixed price $62 per person.

What to See

The Brick Store Museum, 117 Main St., Kennebunk. 207-
985-4802. Open Tuesday-Saturday 10-4:30. (www.cybertours.
com/brickstore)

Kennebunkport Historical Society, Pasco House, 125
North St., Kennebunkport. 207-967-2751. Exhibitions on
local history. Open year-round Wednesday-Friday 10-4. An-
other property operated by the historical society: The Nott
House, 8 Maine St., Kennebunkport. It is an 1853 Greek Re-
vival house with original furnishings, including wallpaper
and tapestry carpets. Open mid-June to early October Tues-
day-Friday. $5, children under 12 $3.

A Jewel of a Peninsula

Head Just South of Bath to the Phippsburg Peninsula

AIMING TO BEAT THE BOOM-BOX AND COCONUT-OIL crowd at their own game, on summer Saturdays we often rise before the sun and pack our kids, Maggie and Jack, off to Popham Beach State Park in Phippsburg. As the crow flies, Popham Beach, which lies at the mouth of the Kennebec River, is only 25 miles from the bustling college town we call home — and yet just reaching Phippsburg always feels a bit like an adventure.

That's because Phippsburg reposes on 28.2 square miles of rugged forested peninsula, a sober deacon's chin of land jutting into the waters of the New Meadows and Kennebec rivers and Casco Bay. The town has at least a dozen separate villages within its established borders and no clearly defined commercial center. Its complex ecosystem embraces bald eagles, Indian burial grounds, rare dune formations, pristine salt marshes, and enough seafaring history and spirited local chauvinism to fill a town ten times its size.

Phippsburg Center Village is home to handsome salt farms and stark white Colonials, a tidy village library, a

Guests at the Galen C. Moses House may play this 1895 Kimball piano located in the west end of the double parlor. (courtesy Galen C. Moses House)

historical museum housed in an 1859 one-room school-house, and a Congregational church, whose lawn is shaded by an enormous English linden that arborists think was living during the American Revolution. From the near distance, framed by sea, river, and a freshwater pond, its white steeple rising above rooflines older than the U.S. Constitution, Center Village imparts the timelessness of an English pastoral print.

And yet that's just the surface of Phippsburg. Hidden from view from the winding state road to Popham are other villages, tucked into the hills and coves of the peninsula and bearing names like Parker Head and Sebasco, West Point and Winnegance, Co.'s Head, Dormer, Meadowbrook, and Small Point. Phippsburg has at least 80 cemeteries filled with family names that precede the founding of the Republic — and what may be more surprising these days is that many descendants of those families are still here, alive and kicking.

The current population of Phippsburg is about 1,830, approximately what it was in 1850 when the Minotts and Bowkers launched full-rigged ships and schooners here. The shipyards that made Phippsburg thrive in the mid-1800s are long gone, of course, but the elements that made Phippsburg so desirable then — namely its stunning juxtaposition with the sea — remain a source of Phippsburg's pride.

I'll never forget the day that Maggie first laid eyes on the place. We'd arrived three hours before the park's official opening and parked on the shoulder of the road facing one of Phippsburg's vast salt marshes, paused to watch a great blue heron toil for his breakfast, then hoofed our way across the parking lot to the wooden boardwalk leading over the dunes to the beach.

The beach roses were blooming, the air sweet and calm. Maggie tugged me impatiently up the boardwalk until we crested the dune, at which point, as if by director's cue, the beach appeared, the sun rose, and my daughter's face shone rapturous with discovery.

She released my hand and bolted like a fiddler crab for

the gently nuzzling surf. I caught her at water's edge. She grinned at the famous rock island just offshore (called Fox Island and happily reachable on foot at low tide), abruptly pirouetted, and extended her small arms as if to embrace the blessed sweet perfection of sand and sea and sky.

"Look, Daddy," she declared. "It's all mines!"

For almost 400 years, explorers like my daughter have aspired to claim this rugged, thin-soiled, pine-thatched extension of land necklaced by spectacular sand beaches as their very own place.

A Less Crowded Beach

Tom Church, owner of Coveside B&B, shares some local knowledge: A beautiful stretch of beach that tends to be less crowded than Popham is Reid State Park, where you'll find a mile and a half of sand with rocky headlands. After the Bath Bridge, turn south on Route 127, and in about ten miles look for the right turn into Reid State Park. Tom says the prettiest lobster dock can be found a couple of miles beyond Reid State Park in the village of Five Islands. At Five Islands Lobster Company you'll find fresh lobster in all forms, chowder, steamers, corn, ice cream, and grilled meats and fish.

His suggestion for working off the lobster roll: Take the two-mile hike on a dirt road up Morse Mountain to a very private beach. To get there, take Route 209 south (but don't take the left to Popham), and stay on this road, which becomes Route 216 (Small Point Road). You'll find the Bates-Morse Mountain Conservation Area on your left. Look for cars parked along the side of the road.

Five Islands Lobster Company, directions in the words of the manager: "Take Route 127 to the end or until your hat floats." 207-371-2990. Open Mother's Day-Columbus Day daily 11-8 (shorter hours in autumn). $-$$.

Certainly the two boatloads of 100 male British settlers who archeologists say put in on the rocky shores of Atkins Bay in August 1607, three months after a similar expedition arrived at Jamestown, Virginia, must have felt the place was all theirs, too. Under the direction of Sir George Popham, they set about constructing an elaborate "palisaded entrenched fort," as well as cutting down timber for building additional ships. The harsh winter took them by surprise, however, and sickness and disillusionment did in their lofty ambitions. With the death of Sir George and waning interest from sponsors back home, the surviving settlers climbed aboard their vessels and headed back to England. The settlement never materialized. However, the strategic importance of the site, located at the mouth of an aboriginal highway into the heart of the northern wilderness, and the legacy of shipbuilding established by Popham and crew meant the place was destined to evolve.

By the War of 1812, the mere sight of gun emplacements on Co.'s Head kept a British warship from cruising up the river to lay waste to Bath's thriving shipyards. As the story goes, a teenage sentry, destined to be dubbed "Maine's Paul Revere," galloped a dozen miles to warn Bath's citizenry, who promptly tossed their silverware down their wells and headed for refuge in adjoining Merrymeeting Bay. The British decided not to risk a dash upriver past the gun on Co.'s Head — which was fortunate, because it had no ammunition.

The U.S. government appreciated the importance of the dorsal fin of granite jutting into the mouth of the river when it began constructing Fort Popham there in 1861. The fort was similar in design to Charleston's Fort Sumter, but alas, the advent of more powerful cannons made it obsolete by the Civil War. The fort was manned but never finished. During World Wars I and II, however, Fort Baldwin atop Sabino Hill was manned by coastal artillery units — though no shots were ever fired there in anger, either.

At the turn of the century, thanks to the steamboat and carriage trade from Boston and New York, Popham Beach

Maine Maritime Museum in Bath boasts over 17,000 artifacts, including this exhibit housed in the L.L. Bean Lobstering Building. (courtesy Maine Maritime Museum)

was a popular retreat for the well-to-do and home to several large wooden hotels and guest cottages. There were aims of turning it into another Bar Harbor, but steamboats died, no trains came, and the carriage ride was just a little too long for most folks. The big hotels eventually burned or were torn down. For better or for worse, Phippsburg was left to its natives and the hardier summer folk. And to others, like me, whom some might consider Popham Beach interlopers. I confess I find myself selfishly projecting ahead to other summers and the empty beach of early morning. I see my daughter dancing as joyously as a sylph in the new sunlight at the water's edge and say quietly to myself, "It's mines. All mines."

– *James Dodson*

Editors' Picks for the Bath-Brunswick Region

General Information

Chamber of Commerce of the Bath-Brunswick Region, 45 Front St., Bath, ME 04530. 207-443-9751. (horton.col.k12.me.us/ccbbr)

Where to Stay

Coveside Bed & Breakfast, North End Rd., HC 33, P.O. Box 462, Georgetown, ME 04548. 800-232-5490, 207-371-2807. All rooms have a view down the lawn to a small cove and beyond to Sheepscot Bay. Two units are housekeeping suites. Canoe and bicycles are available for guest use. Private baths available in each of six rooms. Open mid-May to Columbus Day. Breakfast included. $95-$140. (www.gwi.net/coveside)

Fairhaven Inn, North Bath Rd., RR 2, P.O. Box 85, Bath, ME 04530. 888-443-4391, 207-443-4391. A 1790 Colonial situated on 17 acres, where meadow meets tidal creek; three working fireplaces; lots of woods for quiet country walks; X-C skiing in winter. Eight rooms; (six of which have private baths; the other two share a bath). Open year-round. Breakfast included. $60-$120. (www.mainecoast.com/fairhaveninn)

The Galen C. Moses House, 1009 Washington St., Bath, ME 04530. 888-442-8771, 207-442-8771. An 1874 vernacular Italianate-style home on one acre, surrounded by bountiful gardens; antiques, working fireplace, cozy library, and piano; listed on the National Register of Historic Houses. Four rooms, three with private baths. Open year-round. Breakfast included. $69-$99. (www.galenmoses.com)

The Inn at Bath, 969 Washington St., Bath, ME 04530. 207-443-4294. An 1810 Greek Revival home in the picturesque and quiet historic district. One block from the Kennebec River and a short walk to shops and restaurants. All guest rooms have private baths, air-conditioning, cable television, VCRs, telephones; first-floor handicapped-accessible guest room built to ADA specs with outdoor access ramp. Five rooms contain wood-burning fireplaces; two rooms have two-person Jacuzzis overlooking the fireplace. Open year-round. Breakfast included. $85-$165. (www.innatbath.com)

Benjamin F. Packard House, 45 Pearl St., Bath, ME 04530. 800-516-4578, 207-443-6069. A 1790 Georgian with Victorian decor; located in the heart of Bath's historic district; former home to five generations of noted shipbuilder Benjamin F. Packard; walled garden and private parlor both available for use; near Maine Maritime Museum, beaches, and restaurants. Three rooms with private baths. Open year-round. Breakfast included. $65-$90. (www.mainecoast.com/packardhouse/)

Where to Eat

Kennebec Tavern & Marina, 119 Commercial St., Bath. 207-442-9636. Something here for everybody — seafood, steak, chicken, and pasta. Staff are quoted as saying they serve "good homemade food and lots of it, doing it the Maine way, on the water." Desserts made on premises. Open year-round daily for lunch and dinner. $$-$$$.

Beale Street Barbeque & Grill, 215 Water St., Bath. 207-442-9514. Another local favorite for tasty pork and ribs. Fish and great sandwiches also available. Open year-round daily for lunch and dinner. $$.

J. R. Maxwell's, 122 Front St., Bath. 207-443-2014. Long-standing favorite with families for a wide variety of dishes from hamburgers to steaks, veal, prime rib, and seafood. Open year-round daily for lunch and dinner. $-$$.

Kristina's, 160 Center St., Bath. 207-442-8577. You can't miss at this bakery turned sophisticated eatery. Great fish entrées, quiche, chicken pot pie, and more. Bread and pastry available from the perennially popular bakery. Open high season Monday-Saturday 8 A.M.-9 P.M., Sunday 9-2; off-season hours vary (call ahead). $$.

What to See

Maine Maritime Museum, 243 Washington St., Bath. 207-443-1316. Here you will see over a million artifacts relating to Maine's shipbuilding and fishing heritage. Don't miss narrated cruises (not included in admission price), lighthouse tours ($30 for daylong cruise, members $25), and other special shorter cruises. Open year-round, except major holidays 9:30-5. $8, seniors $7.20, children under 17 $5.50, under 6 free, family maximum $24. (www.bathmaine.com)

Mount Deserted

Joys of Acadia National Park in Winter

IT TAKES WHAT POET WALLACE STEVENS CALLED "a mind of winter" to enjoy Maine's Acadia National Park in January. Come to Acadia National Park in January or February, or any winter month, when less than one percent of the year's three million park visitors pass through. It is colder then, but at least you can have the illusion that all this beauty is yours alone.

I drove through the deserted streets of Bar Harbor on a Friday night in February, through the snow whipping across the street. In season the hotels are regularly full, but on this coldest weekend of the year I had my pick of several.

The next morning I saw the reflected brilliance of sunrise on an empty bay. A misty fog hung on the water, and above it the Porcupine Islands spread out in a bristling half circle. Behind them, on the mainland, stood Mount Battie. Snow had drifted against the stems of brittle weeds on the shore in scalloped swirls.

It's easy to imagine why French explorer Samuel de Champlain took one look at the bareness of the island's mountaintops while sailing its shores in 1604 and named it l'Isle des Monts-déserts, Mount Desert Island. On a map Mount Desert looks like a brain, the two hemispheres separated by Somes Sound. Somes is the only fjord on the Atlantic coast, and in winter it's a favorite spot of ice climbers from the University of Maine.

Others, who like to hike and ski, flock to the eastern part of the island, where most of the trails and carriage roads lie. The 45 miles of carriage roads, designed by John D. Rockefeller Jr., are wide, gently sloped paths with stunning views of Somes Sound and the Atlantic beyond; of Jordan Pond, Bubble Pond, or Eagle Lake; of Blue Hill Bay; of Cadillac Mountain; and of frozen creeks, trees, and sky. They pass through the ice-coated poplar and birch that grew up after the great fire of 1947 destroyed much of the spruce and fir forest.

I skied through some of that forest, from Parkman Mountain to Jordan Pond, and then back again. It took me most of the morning. In that time I saw only two people, but tracks of deer and fox and snowshoe hare were everywhere, and on the edge of Jordan Pond I found the cradle of an otter slide. The first stretch of Park Loop Road was plowed, and that night the full moon shone so brightly on the snow-covered roadside that I drove with my headlights off to Sand Beach.

South of Sand Beach on the Loop Road lies Thunder Hole. Stairs lead from the road to an observation deck at sea level. In summer, tourists crowd the railing to snap pictures of the ocean spouting from a boulder cave. The spume is biggest during a three-quarter rising tide with a rough sea, but nature offers no guarantees when the big one will be.

One August a high surf shot a 14-foot spray out of Thunder Hole, and tourists from all over stacked the Park Road. Extra staffers were called in to keep people back. "There are so many tourists at Thunder Hole today," said one ranger, "that the island is about to tilt."

In winter, when the seas are rougher and the waves wash the observation deck out of sight, the Thunder Hole show is even more spectacular, but no one's there to see it. The ocean leaps the rail and sprays the Loop Road with beautiful, lethal ice. Perhaps it's just as well that the tourists have gone, for four-fifths of the park staff have left for the winter as well. It is then that the locals return to claim their

Waterfall Bridge, built in 1925, is one of 16 carriage-road bridges in Acadia National Park. (photo by Kevin Shields, courtesy Bar Harbor Chamber of Commerce)

prized park. They come to cross-country ski and hike and snowmobile through Acadia's nearly 40,000 acres.

Bar Harbor is considered the gateway and the most popular town in season. But Bar Harbor in winter is like any organism responding to cold: It closes in on itself, shutting down the extremities (like thousands of guest rooms), keeping the community core intact. One winter several years ago, things got so quiet that the weekly police blotter was short: "Southwest Harbor police reported all was quiet last week. Except for Tuesday, when a Forest Avenue woman phoned police to complain about a neighbor's dog who repeatedly stole cat food off her porch."

In 1796 Bar Harbor belonged to Massachusetts, and the government there chose to call it Eden in honor of an Englishman. Locals, being more practical, called it Bar Harbor because of the sandbar that connects Mount Desert to Bar Island at low tide. After 125 years the government finally gave in and officially changed the name to Bar Harbor.

It was in the 1820s and 1830s that Bar Harbor became a playground for yachtsmen who hiked and climbed and hunted in the forest. And it was the artwork of landscape painters Thomas Cole and Frederic Church in the mid-1800s that attracted others to Eden. The tourists then were known as "rusticators" or "summercators." They were put up at first by local families, but as more came over the years by train and boat from Boston, Philadelphia, Washington, Chicago, and all over, hotels sprang up and grew in number and size until they hit 30 in 1880, including one atop Cadillac Mountain and one (the Rodick House) that was the biggest summer hotel in the country. Clearly Mount Desert was the place to be in summer; wealthy families — the Rockefellers, Vanderbilts, Pulitzers, Morgans, Astors — all built lavish cottages. To make sure the island stayed the way they liked it, many of those prominent families contributed to the creation of Acadia National Park. Under the leadership of Charles Eliot and George Bucknam Dorr, the rusticators put together a land trust at the turn of the century and in 1916 officially established the first national park east of the Mississippi. It was also the first national park formed entirely of land donated by private citizens.

I drove to the base of Cadillac Mountain. In summer the summit road is often bumper-to-bumper, but now the unplowed road made a perfect path for my ascent on skis. It took me the rest of the morning, with frequent stops to view the interior of the island and Eastern Bay, but it was a splendid way to spend a sunny winter's day. At the top, 1,530 feet, I had reached the park's highest spot — the highest spot on the Atlantic coast north of Brazil. If I had made it here at dawn, I could've been the first in the country to see the sun's

---

WHAT THE **LOCALS KNOW**

Mount Desert's Best View

Bill Haefele, who works for the Mount Desert Island Information Center, has lived in the area for 25 years. He notes that visitors often overlook a spectacular view of the island — the view from the outer islands. "When you come on the island, you see one side of the mountains and from the water another," he says. "Nowhere else on the East Coast will you see mountains meet the ocean like this." He recommends taking one of the following mail-boat trips: Cranberry Cove Boating Company or Beal & Bunker, which runs the mail boat and ferry service year-round to the Cranberry Islands, Islesford, and in the summer to Sutton Island. Bill says he can't count the number of people who have come back to thank him for this advice. (Even veteran visitors to Mount Desert say this is their favorite thing to do.)

Cranberry Cove Boating Company, Southwest Harbor. 207-244-5882. Call for tour times. $12, children 6 and under $6.

Beal & Bunker, Northeast Harbor. 207-244-3575. Round-trip $10.

rays. It is also the island's best lookout: To the east lie the islands of Frenchman Bay with the Schoodic Peninsula beyond, to the south the Cranberry Islands, Seal Harbor, and the open sea.

You might think Cadillac Mountain was named for the well-paved road up its side, but it was named for Antoine de la Mothe Cadillac, who took possession of the island in the late 1600s and later founded Detroit. If Cadillac Mountain were a Cadillac car, it would be pink, as is the granite underfoot — pink feldspar, glassy quartz, and blackish hornblende. My ski to the bottom passed in one long, continuous schuss. It matched the best backcountry skiing I have ever done.

That night I camped at the Blackwoods Campground on the southern tip of the island — as peaceful a night as I can remember. In the morning I snowshoed through the deserted park to the water's edge and watched the sun rise on the Atlantic. I must admit that I felt clever to have such a sight to myself. Now that I have been to Acadia in winter, I may never go back in summer again.

– *Michael Burke*

Editors' Picks for Bar Harbor and Mount Desert

General Information

Mount Desert Island Information Center at Thompson Island, Rte. 3, P.O. Box 396, Bar Harbor, ME 04609. 207-288-3411. Open mid-May to mid-October.

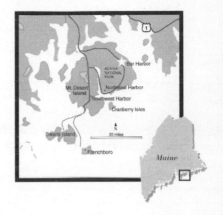

Southwest Harbor Tremont Chamber of Commerce, Main St., P.O. Box 1143, Southwest Harbor, ME 04679. 800-423-9264, 207-244-9264. Open year-round. (www.acadia.net/swhtrcoc)

Bar Harbor Chamber, 93 Cottage St., P.O. Box 158, Bar Harbor, ME 04609. 800-288-5103, 207-288-5103. Open year-round. (www.barharborinfo.com)

Where to Stay

The Bar Harbor Chamber has a complete list of year-round lodgings; here are just a few where we've stayed.

Atlantic Oakes by the Sea, 119 Eden St., P.O. Box 3, Bar Harbor, ME 04609. 800-336-2463, 207-288-5801. The Atlantic Oakes is a restored estate mansion that offers an attractive coastal setting with views of Frenchman Bay from nearly every room. The 153-room complex includes a B&B with eight rooms, each with private bath. The complex is situated on 12 private oceanfront acres, one mile from the village of Bar Harbor and the entrance to Acadia National Park. Five tennis courts; indoor and outdoor pool; whirlpool. Open year-round. Deluxe continental breakfast included in a stay at the B&B part of this complex. $62-$265. (www.barharbor.com)

Graycote Inn, 40 Holland Ave., Bar Harbor, ME 04609. 207-288-3044. A restored 1881 Victorian on a tree-shaded acre lot with lawns, flower gardens, private sunrooms, balconies, and working fireplaces. There are 12 rooms, each with private bath. Many of the queen and king beds have canopies. Located within an easy walk to shops, galleries, and restaurants. Open year-round. Breakfast included. $65-$150. (www.graycoteinn.com)

Harbour Woods B&B and Cottages, 410 Main St., Southwest Harbor, ME 04679. 207-244-5388. An 1840 Maine farmhouse on three-plus acres surrounded by Acadia National Park. The three B&B rooms and 11 cottages all have private baths. B&B rooms have queen beds, fireplaces, in-room telephones, cable TVs, and hot tub. Cottages are nestled in lightly wooded setting and equipped with refreshment or cooking areas and full/queen-size beds. Heated pool on premises. B&B open all year; cottages open May-October. Breakfast included. B&B $75-$99, cottages $59-$99. (www.acadia.net/harbourwoods)

Hatfield Bed & Breakfast, 20 Roberts Ave., Bar Harbor, ME 04609. 207-288-9655. An 1895 Victorian; "Eldorado" on the third floor features a spectacular view of Cadillac Mountain; cozy fireplace in living room; front porch; afternoon refreshments served. This B&B has six rooms, four with private baths; the other two share a bath. Open year-round. Breakfast included. $50-$110. (www.hatfieldinn.com)

Bar Harbor Tides Bed & Breakfast, 119 West St., Bar Harbor, ME 04609. 207-288-4968. An 1887 Greek Revival cottage on the National Register of Historic Places, offering four rooms, each with private bath and two with working fireplaces; suites and veranda have sweeping views of Frenchman Bay; outdoor fireplace on veranda; beautifully landscaped formal gardens. Open year-round. Breakfast included. $95-$275. (www.barharbortides.com)

Where to Eat

Blackboards Restaurant, 101 Cottage St., Bar Harbor. 207-288-9098. Serves all three meals in a relaxed family atmosphere. Favorites include "wrapwiches," which are chicken, wild rice, lettuce, tomato, and salsa wrapped in a tortilla shell. Another popular dish is the Haddock Elizabeth, sautéed with Chardonnay, garlic, tomato, mushroom, and onion, served over wild rice. Open year-round daily 7 A.M.-9 P.M. $-$$.

Café Bluefish, 122 Cottage St., Bar Harbor. 207-288-3696. Chef-owner Bobbie-Lynn Hutchins is a great cook. She is known for her award-winning vegetarian cuisine, but her fish dishes are outstanding. Try curry-crusted salmon, Cajun-crusted swordfish, or another signature dish — lobster strudel. Antique books and mismatched, old-fashioned china create a warm atmosphere. Open (nearly) year-round daily 5:30-10 P.M. Bobbie-Lynn says winter is less predictable, so be sure to call ahead. $$-$$$.

Mama DiMatteo's, 34 Kennebec Pl., Bar Harbor. 207-288-3666. Italian cuisine in a casual atmosphere; all dishes are prepared to order. Specialties include pasta, local seafood, and hand-cut steaks. One of their best-sellers is Tuscan tenderloin — grilled beef crusted with sage, rosemary, and garlic, served with Gorgonzola butter. Open year-round; in summer daily for dinner; in winter Monday-Saturday for dinner. $$.

The Sporting Camps of Maine

The Real Spirit of the Great North Woods

FOR MY MONEY, IF THERE IS ANY ONE THING THAT truly captures the quintessential spirit of Maine, it is the sporting camp, an elegant and isolated retreat at which to fish, hunt, or simply enjoy the beauty and serenity of the Great North Woods.

The Maine sporting camp — which is distinctly and historically different from, say, a camp in the Adirondacks or a Montana fishing camp or a Colorado dude ranch — has classic elements. These include, apart from the traditional infrastructure, a setting in the deep forest; adjacency to a mountain pond of stunning beauty with abundant trout and salmon; and wonderfully diverse wildlife, from moose to white-throated sparrows.

Born more or less after 1844 in the Rangeley Lakes area, and nurtured by railroad expansion and Maine's discovery by America's royalty of the day, the Maine sporting experience achieved its greatest popularity in the Victorian period

Meg Witherbee shows off a 3½-pound landlocked salmon that she caught with the help of Maine Guide Shane Nichols. (*courtesy Cobb's Pierce Pond Camps*)

and lasted to just before World War I.

It is a modest irony, perhaps, that if Benedict Arnold did nothing else for his country, his trek to capture Quebec at the end of 1775, a remarkable feat of woodsmanship and endurance, prepared the way for a virtual superhighway of recreational luxury in the Great North Woods. Members of his battalion saw the potential in the Dead River region in and around Stratton and Eustis. They settled there in later years and relished its remarkable fishing and hunting. Ultimately, in the post–Civil War period, when America's rich discovered that the Maine wilderness had more to offer than blackflies — like truly huge brook trout — there were more than 100 sporting camps in that area.

And then, with the onset of World War I, the boom ended. Although that golden age is gone and there are far fewer camps today, the concept still flourishes, just as rustic, just as elegant, just as serene.

– Spence Conley

Editors' Picks for Our Favorite Sporting Camps

General Information

The Maine Sporting Camp Association, P.O. Box 89, Jay, ME 04239. 207-897-5417. Send for a brochure.

Where to Stay

Among the dozens of excellent camps that operate today from the Rangeleys in the west to Grand Lake Stream in the east, there are a half dozen that stand as the benchmarks of what such camps should be. Here are some of our favorites (rates given are per person per day, including all meals, unless otherwise noted).

Cobb's Pierce Pond Camps, P.O. Box 124, North New Portland, ME 04961. 207-628-2819. Gary Cobb, whose family has run these camps since 1958, has a well-deserved reputation for a quality operation on one of the few ponds in Maine that might very well produce a state-record brook trout. Open May-November. $75, $140 per couple.

Tim Pond Wilderness Camps, P.O. Box 22, Eustis, ME 04936. 207-243-2947, winter 207-897-4056. Started in the mid-1800s, Tim Pond is possibly the oldest continuously operating sporting camp in America, and what has contributed so much to its longevity is a population of wonderful native brook trout (nine to 12 inches), a major concentration of songbirds, white-tailed deer, loons, and moose, as well as the occasional bear. You won't find a more private location than this. Open year-round. $110. (www.timpondcamps.com)

Lakewood Camps, Middledam, Andover, ME 04216. 207-243-2959. Located along the western shore of Lower Richardson Lake, it is another in the Rangeley chain, providing easy access to the Rapid River. It was here in 1844 that the first truly major American brook trout fishery was born. Between Upper Dam, which is at the southern end of Lake Mooselookmeguntic, and Lakewood Camps, which were founded as the Angler's Retreat more than 150 years ago, the sportsmen of the day captured brook trout that often weighed more than ten pounds. (Nowadays they are happily boasting seven pounds.) Open mid-May to October. $95.

Libby Camps, P.O. Box 810, Ashland, ME 04732. 207-435-8274. Farther to the east, between Baxter State Park and the Allagash Wilderness Waterway, is where Matt and Ellen Libby carry on a family tradition that started in 1890. The camps are located along the shore of Millinocket Lake and offer landlocked salmon in addition to brookies for angling guests. Open May-November. $115.

Nugent's Chamberlain Lake Camps, HCR 76, Box 632, Greenville, ME 04441. 207-944-5991. These camps are actually within the boundary of the Allagash Wilderness Waterway, about 60 miles from Millinocket, mostly via logging roads. Here is a solitary spot on 17-mile-long Chamberlain Lake, founded by Al Nugent and Patty Pelkey in 1926. The camps are very rustic; their location inside the Wilderness Waterway requires them to be so. There is no running water, but there is an excellent community bathhouse. Open year-round. Housekeeping cabins $25, modified American plan (includes cabin and dinner) $40, American plan (includes cabin, three meals, and linens) $60. (www.mainerec.com/ nugent-mcnally/)

Packard's Camps, RR 2, Box 176, Guilford, ME 04443. 207-997-3300. Located on Sebec Lake, just outside Guilford, this is something of a compromise between the true wilderness camp and the more easily accessible camp. It offers greater diversity of fishing as well. Along with lake trout and landlocked salmon, there is an excellent fishery for smallmouth bass. Open May-November. $315 per week for two (no meals, but fully equipped kitchens in all camps).

Vermont

Mount Mansfield, Vermont (photo by Radu Manoliu, courtesy Stowe Area Association)

Making Peace with the Battenkill

Fishing Vermont's Fabled River

"Commonly they did not think that they were lucky, or well paid for their time, unless they got a long string of fish, though they had the opportunity of seeing the pond all the while. They might go there a thousand times before the sediment of fishing would sink to the bottom and leave their purpose pure; but no doubt such a clarifying process would be going on all the while."
– HENRY DAVID THOREAU, *Walden*

I HAD FISHED THE BATTENKILL JUST ONCE BEFORE. I had caught nothing and had felt unlucky and poorly paid for my time. I returned 20 years later, determined, this time, to catch a worthy trout on a dry fly and thus make my peace with this fabled Vermont river — an undertaking, I realized, that others considered the work of a lifetime. I had no illusions. Everyone knows the Battenkill is one of the world's most challenging trout streams.

I talked to the clerks at Orvis in Manchester, and the proprietor of the little fly shop over the New York border, and the other anglers I encountered along the river, and even

Hoping to land a fabled Battenkill trout, a student at the Orvis Fly-Fishing School in Manchester, Vermont, practices his casting. (courtesy Orvis)

the groundskeeper at the inn in Arlington where I stayed. One hesitates to ask another fisherman to divulge the location of a hot spot. So I scouted for places where I, if I were a worthy trout, might choose to live. I discovered that the Battenkill has very little water that doesn't look as if it would harbor worthy trout. I also discovered that very few worthy trout live there.

On the first day I explored a section of the river that a young clerk at Orvis called "the Jungle." The sun dappled it here and there as I edged upstream. Warblers flitted in the May foliage, which glowed in vibrant young shades of pale green and yellow. Pink and crimson and white wildflowers sprouted along the riverbank.

I've fished many of America's most beautiful trout rivers — Nelson's and Armstrong's spring creeks in Montana's Paradise Valley, the South Fork of the Snake and the Middle Fork of the Salmon in Idaho, and the limestone creeks of Pennsylvania, not to mention the dozens of little streams that flow through the creases of Vermont's Green Mountains. None is more beautiful than the Battenkill.

A mile and several hours after I had entered the river, I rounded a bend. A long stretch of flat water curved upstream into the jungle. And there against the left bank I saw the widening rings that I had been looking for. I noticed a few caddis flies fluttering above the river; I snatched one and held it in my hand. Tan wings and olive body, about size 16. I found a match in my fly box and knotted it to my tippet. Then I moved into position, merging my rhythm with the fish until I felt he was prepared to rise again. My cast was true. My fly settled softly on the water four feet upstream of him and drifted down, and then it disappeared into the pockmark of his rise.

I tightened on him to set the hook. And then I laughed aloud. With the lift of my nine-foot rod, the fish came skittering across the surface of the water toward me. I stripped him in and held him in my hand. With his tail against the base of my thumb, his nose barely extended beyond my fingertips. A six-incher, by the fisherman's generous estimate. An altogether tiny trout.

But I had the good sense to admire him. He glittered in my hand like a gold nugget, perfectly camouflaged for the river bottom where he lived. His red spots glowed like droplets of fresh blood. He was a perfect miniature of the worthy brown trout I sought. Nowadays a wild New England trout, however tiny, is always a miracle. Only a lout would fail to pause to admire one of them before slipping him gently back into the river.

I explored the loop of river between the first two bridges on Route 313 in Arlington on the second day. I saw no rising trout. I spent most of the day sitting on streamside boulders, watching sunlight ricochet off the riffles. For all I could tell, not a trout lived in this Battenkill pool, yet I was reluctant to leave. Swallows had begun to swoop close to the water, and a few caddis flies swarmed in the air.

Then I saw the rise of a trout, and as I watched, I saw two more. One of them appeared to be heftier than my six-incher. As dusk gathered, the fish began to feed more hungrily. Now I had at least a dozen actively rising fish in front of me. I cast frantically, amateurishly, first to this one, and then, when another rose nearby, I'd interrupt the drift of my fly, lift my line, and cast to him. Perhaps some of these were worthy trout, although I couldn't judge.

Then I caught one. He did not come skittering in over the surface, but neither did he slog heavily at the end of my line. I landed him easily and measured him against the markings on my rod. His nose failed by an inch to reach the one-foot mark. He was a brook trout, a species native to the Battenkill. Perhaps this one was a descendant of those that settled here after the glaciers retreated. More likely his ancestors were hatchery trout that were heavily stocked a century ago.

In Arlington the river takes a right turn and flows east to west into New York, where, for some reason, they call it the Batten Kill. On the third day I prowled this stretch, which for several miles meanders between Route 313 and a dirt road.

In the morning, as I sat on the riverbank watching the water, a hen turkey ambled to the water's edge across from me. I didn't move, but she saw me anyway and ran awkwardly into the bushes. Toward dusk a whitetail doe waded into the head of the pool I was fishing. In between, I caught two miniature brown trout and one finger-size brookie. I guessed that all three, laid head to tail, would barely stretch beyond the length of my 11-inch brookie. I had again avoided being skunked.

But I had not encountered the worthy trout I sought. I knew they lived here. The largest brown trout ever taken from the Battenkill weighed over 12 pounds. But that happened 50 years ago. After three days on the river, I had seen enough to understand that the Battenkill has the potential to match some of the most productive trout waters I have fished. Its pure water — a mix from the springs that rise in the Taconics to the west and warmer surface runoff from the Green Mountains to the east — rarely exceeds 70 degrees, which is ideal for brown trout and tolerable for brookies. The alkaline riverbed encourages weed and insect growth. Trout reproduce abundantly here. But they are overfished and overharvested and undermanaged.

By the fourth day I figured the best chance to encounter my worthy brown trout lay in a four-mile stretch over the New York border. Rain clouds obscured the mountains, and mist hung over the river. The air was still and heavy and damp. A good day for insects. A good day for a worthy brown trout to come out to eat them. A good day for a fly fisherman. I sat on a rock. Here, I decided, I would take my stand. I would sit here all day, if necessary, to wait for him to show himself.

A ring appeared near the tailout, not 30 feet from me. I could cast to him without moving. Gradually more rings began to appear and an hour passed before I saw the unmistakable black nose. On the Henry's Fork and the Bighorn I learned to measure a surface-feeding trout by the size of his nose. We call the big ones "toads" because that's what their noses look like against the water.

Here on the Battenkill I had found a toad. After three days, the Battenkill had showed me a worthy trout. Now it was up to me. I had to resist the impulse to cast. I was still too far from him. One careless presentation would spook him. A hollow thunk echoed from somewhere upstream, but it barely registered. I was focused on my trout. I was almost there.

Then the man in the canoe materialized out of the mist. He paddled placidly down the middle of my pool, directly over the place where my trout had been rising.

"Any luck?" he asked cheerfully. I shook my head. "Nope." "Say," he said, "you got the time?" I glanced at my watch. "Three-fifteen." "Thanks." He waved. "Well, good luck, then."

I watched the canoe's bow waves roll toward the banks. The canoe became a shadow before the mist enveloped it. Three-fifteen. I had parked at the covered bridge at nine. In effect, I had been stalking that toad for over six hours. I waded carelessly back to the car. There was no need to worry about my waves spooking fish. Every worthy trout in the river had been sent scurrying by that one man in his canoe.

That evening the river ran dark and deep along a granite ledge overhung by hemlocks. It was beautiful and peaceful in the mist, and I spotted the rings of a few rising trout and caught two of them — five or six inches long, beautiful miniature Battenkill brown trout. I fished until dark, casting rhythmically, no longer in search of a worthy trout, and finally the sediment of fishing sank to the bottom and my purpose became pure. And so I made my peace with the Battenkill.

– William G. Tapply

Editors' Picks for Manchester and Beyond

General Information

Manchester in the Mountains, Main St., Manchester, VT 05255. 802-362-2100. (www.manchesterandmtns.com)

Orvis Fly-Fishing School, Rte. 7A, Manchester, VT 05254. 800-235-9763, 802-362-3622. The Orvis schools are located at the corporate headquarters and store. Courses run April-October. $395 includes instruction, use of equipment, lunches, and Vermont fishing license for 2½-day course.

Where to Stay and Eat

Arlington Inn, Vermont Historic Rte. 7A, Arlington, VT 05250. 800-443-9442, 802-375-6532. Dream of worthy trout at this 1848 Greek Revival mansion on over three acres, featuring fireplaces, antiques-filled rooms, fireplaced dining room, and formal parlor. Nineteen rooms with private baths. Open year-round. Full country breakfast included. $70-$205. Special packages available. (www.discoververmont.com/Banner/arlington.htm)

The Equinox, Historic Rte. 7A, Manchester, VT 05254. 800-362-4747, 802-362-4700. This 163-room inn is a rambling labyrinth of 17 distinct parts, with over 220 years of history. Victorian visitors once rocked on the endless colonnaded porch; many of today's patrons would rather be on the superb 18-hole golf course (restored to Scottish championship standards) or fishing for trout in the stocked 14-acre pond. Open year-round. $179-$319. Marsh Tavern open daily for lunch and light-fare dinner; $-$$$. Colonnade dining room open Tuesday-Saturday for dinner, reservations suggested; $$$-$$$$. (www.equinoxresort.com)

Inn at West View Farm, Rte. 30, Dorset, VT 05251. 800-769-4903, 802-867-5715. This serene, relaxing circa 1870 farmhouse surrounded by mountains is just the place to unwind after a day on the Battenkill. It offers ten rooms with private baths. Open year-round. Breakfast included. $85-$140. Auberge Room open daily 6-9 P.M. for fine dining. $$$-$$$$. Clancy's Tavern open daily 6-9 P.M. for casual fare. (www.vtweb.com/innatwestviewfarm)

The Inn at Willow Pond, Box 1429, Manchester Center, VT 05255. 800-533-3533, 802-362-4733. Situated on 20 scenic acres with panoramic mountain views, this is a favorite retreat among anglers. Rooms and suites feature marble baths, handmade quilts, and fireplaces. $138-$208. Meal plans and special packages (including hunting and fishing with Orvis Fly-Fishing School) available. Northern Italian cuisine served in restored 1770s farmhouse 5:30-9:30 P.M. $$-$$$.

Hill Farm Inn, Hill Farm Rd., Sunderland, VT 05250. 800-882-2545, 802-375-2269. Enjoy mountain views at this farmhouse inn, guest house, and cabins on 50 acres, including a mile of frontage on Battenkill. Open year-round; cabins open May-October. Full breakfast included. $65-$150. Four-course fixed-price dinner $35 per couple, available by reservation. (www.hillfarminn.com)

What to See

The American Museum of Fly-Fishing, Seminary Ave. and Rte. 7A, Manchester Village. 802-362-3300. Here you can see rods and reels made and owned by famous people, as well as an extensive display of the lovely flies of Mary Orvis Marbury. Open year-round 10-4. $3, children and members free.

Equinox Skyline Drive, south of Manchester Village, Rte. 7A. 802-362-1114. Southern Vermont's best summit drive snakes to the top of 3,840-foot Mount Equinox. Views take in the Green Mountains, Berkshires, Adirondacks, and under perfect conditions, New Hampshire's Mount Washington and faraway Mount Royal in Montreal. Summit hiking trails range up to two miles. Open early May-October. Driver $6, passengers over 12 $2.

Hildene, Rte. 7A, Manchester. 802-362-1788. Vermont isn't really mansion country, but this Georgian Revival great house built by Robert Todd Lincoln, the president's son, is a handsome exception. The 24-room home is filled with Lincoln family furnishings and heirlooms. Grounds open mid-May to October daily 9:30-5:30 (last tour begins at 4 P.M.). Cross-country skiing beginning in December. Candlelight tours December 27-29. $7, children 6-14 $3, under 6 free.

Norman Rockwell Exhibition, Rte. 7A, Arlington. 888-443-7353, 802-375-6423. Small-town America's great chronicler lived in this small town for 14 years; today his one-time models (with a few gray hairs) show you around an 1875 church filled with Rockwell prints. Open daily; November-April 10-4; May-October 9-5; closed January. $2, children under 12 free.

Landscape of Departures and Returns

A Spectacle of Snow Geese in Middlebury

BEGINNING IN EARLY SEPTEMBER, THE WORLD'S most vivid fall colors wash over our northern New England village. Middlebury is the shiretown for Addison County, whose numerous dairy farms and orchards make it one of Vermont's prime agricultural regions. The brilliant sugar maples of the Green Mountains rise around a world of fattening cornfields, reddening apples, and other fulfillments of the season. And just at this spectacular moment, the new crop of Middlebury College students also comes in.

In a college town like ours, the minivans with their roof racks, turning off Route 7 to Main Street and then up College Street to the campus, make their own distinctive contribution to the excitement of fall. There's a jolt of energy into the commercial establishments and community organizations, a noticeable increase of joggers and bikers on the road out to the Morgan Horse Farm. Students coming for the first time always seem to be in constant motion — keenly aware, as they are, of simultaneously beginning a college career and starting an independent life. Those who are returning to Vermont feel increasingly that, wherever they originally came from and wherever they head after graduation, this is now their home.

The season is abundantly celebrated at the college, from a harvest festival on the campus lawns to concerts and readings in the Center for the Arts, to athletic contests on fields a little farther out Route 30. But for me the most exhilarating marker of the fall remains the appearance of wild geese in the skies above our town. Addison County is on a major flyway, with thousands of these spectacular birds pausing to rest and feed in a wildlife sanctuary to our west, ironically named Dead Creek.

Most years there are geese here from late September through early November, with the greatest concentrations around the third week in October. Canada geese arrive in majestic wedges, en route from northern Quebec and Labrador to Chesapeake Bay. As many as 4,000 may be seen at Dead Creek in a given season, their muted brown-gray plumage and the black-white-black of their heads and necks making an elegant pattern against the fields of bleached stubble.

But the snow geese present an even more amazing spectacle as they arrive in their disorderly, gabbling profusion. Upwards of 10,000 pass through Dead Creek annually, as they make their way southward from Ellesmere and the other islands north of Hudson Bay. The feathers of these "greater snow geese" are pure white except for a stark band of black at the tips of each wing. When they rise out of these Vermont fields for their morning and afternoon fly-abouts, the sky fills with the scintillating light of their wings and echoes with their calls.

I especially like going to see the geese with my students from Middlebury College. It's a phenomenon that amazes them and engages them in the seasonal tides that sweep around their college town. Invariably students respond in a strongly personal way to the odyssey of the geese. At this time of their lives, especially, their imaginations rise up with these birds of passage. As the semester gets underway and Vermont's fall gathers toward harvest in the fields, they know that they, too, are at one crucial staging point in a long journey.

– John Elder

Each year upwards of 10,000 snow geese may pass through the Dead Creek Wildlife Management Area, a major flyway near Middlebury. *(photo by Alan Jakubek)*

WHAT THE
LOCALS
KNOW

A Rhyming Ramble

Yankee is one of the few magazines that regularly publishes poetry. Every month we set aside a page for this purpose. And every month we get letters (often from our Maine subscribers) scolding us for publishing poetry that doesn't rhyme. It's not that we don't like rhyming poetry; it just doesn't seem to be in favor among writers these days. Perhaps this is because no one wishes to be compared to our favorite rhyming poet of all, Robert Frost.

Since Frost lived in both New Hampshire *and* Vermont, neither can claim him solely, so both claim him vehemently. Vermont stakes its claim eloquently on one of the prettiest roads in the state. The breathtaking drive through Middlebury Gap is punctuated by a rhyming ramble, the Robert Frost Interpretive Trail.

The easy, mile-long path wends through forests and pastures and crosses wooden footbridges. Along the way, Frost's nature-inspired poems are posted in appropriate settings. "A Young Birch" is framed by a backdrop of birches. "Going for Water" is set to the music of a stream. The view of Breadloaf Mountain pulsates to the rhythm of "A Passing Glimpse." There's another kind of poetry here, too: All the flora are labeled.

I like to hike here in the fall, when the Green Mountains seem shockingly misnamed. I pause for a long while at Frost's "Nothing Gold Can Stay," drenched in warm sunlight bouncing off red and orange leaves, and I read the last lines of the poem aloud: "Then leaf subsides to leaf, so Eden sank to grief, so dawn goes down to day. Nothing gold can stay." A fitting (and rhyming) farewell to fall.

The Robert Frost Interpretive Trail, take Rte. 125 6.5 miles east out of Middlebury to the trailhead and parking lot on the right side of the road.   – *Carol Connare*

Editors' Picks for Middlebury

General Information

Middlebury College
Events: Call the Student Activities office at 802-443-3100.

To See the Geese: Drive eight miles west of Middlebury on Rte. 125, turn north on Rte. 22A for seven miles, then go west on Rte. 17 for a mile and a half. On the left side of the road is a pull-off at an elevated vantage point excellent for viewing the geese. Late mornings and late afternoons are likely times for large flights to be taking off and returning.

Where to Stay

Middlebury Inn, 14 Courthouse Sq., Middlebury, VT 05753. 800-842-4666, 802-388-4961. This 1827 brick hostelry offers gracious public rooms and comfortable accommodations along with a respectable table, right near the center of the picturesque college town. Ask for an upper-floor room in the main building. Open year-round. Continental breakfast and afternoon tea included. $90-$260. Dining rooms open daily for breakfast, lunch, and dinner. $$-$$$. (www.middleburyinn.com)

Waybury Inn, Rte. 125, East Middlebury, VT 05740. 800-348-1810, 802-388-4015. The Waybury Inn sits at the foot of the Green Mountains in the village of East Middlebury.

You may recognize the exterior of the Waybury as the "Stratford Inn" on the popular Bob Newhart series. The inn offers 14 guest rooms, all with private baths. Open year-round. Continental breakfast included. $80-$115. Open nightly for dinner; Sunday brunch 11-2. $$-$$$. (www.wayburyinn.com)

Brookside Meadows Inn, RD #3 Box 2460, Painter Rd., Middlebury, VT 05753. 800-442-9887, 802-388-6429. Set on a quiet country road three miles from the center of Middlebury, this comfortable B&B offers five rooms, including two suites, all with private baths. The common room overlooks lawn, garden, meadow, and mountains. Open year-round. Breakfast included. $85-$135. (www.brooksmeadow.com)

Swift House Inn, 25 Stewart Lane, Middlebury, VT 05753. 802-388-9925. The mansion home of Jessica Stewart Swift is now open as an inn, with rooms in the 1814 Main House, Victorian Gate House, and the 1886 Carriage House. Some have whirlpools, private balconies, and fireplaces. Open year-round. Continental breakfast included. $80-$195. Café Swift House open daily for dinner. $$-$$$. (www.swifthouseinn.com)

Where to Eat

Woody's, 5 Bakery Ln., Middlebury. 802-388-4182. This art deco eatery overlooks Otter Creek. Try salad and quiche for lunch, but dig in to daring creations for dinner. You'll find something perfect to sip among the extensive wine and beer lists. Open daily 11:30 A.M.-midnight. $-$$.

Mr. Up's, Bakery Lane Plaza, Middlebury. 802-388-6724. As long as weather permits, tables are set on a deck by the river, the perfect place to snack on nachos or Norwegian salmon. Open daily 11:30 A.M.-midnight. $-$$.

What to See

Vermont State Crafts Center at Frog Hollow, One Mill St., Middlebury. 802-388-3177. One stroll through this gallery reveals what a magnet for fine artisans Vermont has become; the beautifully displayed stock includes jewelry, ceramics, textiles, furniture, glass, and more. That gorgeous picture of the Otter Creek Falls is not for sale, though; it's the view through the back window. Open Memorial Day-Columbus Day Monday-Saturday 9:30-6, Sunday 11-5; after Columbus Day, Monday-Saturday 10-5. (www.froghollow.org)

Vermont Book Shop, 38 Main St., Middlebury. 800-287-2061, 802-388-2061. Vermont independent bookselling is alive and well at this downtown emporium near the Middlebury College campus. There's a fine selection of Vermontiana, and Robert Frost, a longtime customer, is well represented on the shelves. Open year-round, Monday-Saturday 8:30-5:30, Sunday 11-4.

Honeymoon at a Vanderbilt Mansion

The Inn at Shelburne Farms

ON THE DAY AFTER OUR WEDDING, LAURA AND I could already look back on the event with happiness and contentment. Not everything had gone according to plan, but our ceremony and reception had been everything we'd hoped for.

Our honeymoon, however, was not starting out on the right foot. I had arranged to stay at a Vermont inn on our way to the Adirondacks. A friend from Burlington recommended it. We drove north in our leaky convertible. It was chilly, and storm clouds on the horizon were dark and menacing. As Laura asked me more about the surprise honeymoon I'd planned, I grimly admitted I knew almost nothing about the place.

When we came to the imposing stone gates of Shelburne Farms, I wasn't sure I had the right place. As we drove through the misty darkness, the dirt drive was leading us alternately through field and forest. I was starting to look for a spot to turn around when we rounded a corner and saw the lights of what had to be the inn, stretching out along the horizon.

A fire burning in a six-foot-high fireplace greeted us as we walked in. Guests sat around the fire in overstuffed velvet chairs. The giant hall was paneled entirely in golden oak; a three-foot-high vase of fresh flowers stood on a carved wooden table. This, we thought, was no ordinary B&B.

It turns out that the Inn at Shelburne Farms is a Vanderbilt mansion, the home of Lila Vanderbilt Webb and

This 60-room Queen Anne-style mansion, now the Inn at Shelburne Farms, was the home of William Seward and Lila Vanderbilt Webb. (*photo by Del Keppelman*)

*The Marble Dining Room at the Inn at Shelburne
Farms is known for wonderful meals, a roaring fire,
and an elegant marble floor. (photo by Gary Hall)*

William Seward Webb. At the end of the 19th century, they
bought up 30 small farms along the shore of Lake Champlain and created a 4,000-acre estate of their own. First they
built a five-story barn topped with a clock tower that housed
mules, grain, and administrative offices. Next was a barn of
almost equal proportions for horse breeding. Under the direction of Frederick Law Olmsted, the famous landscape architect, hundreds of workers planted thousands of trees on
the estate.

The Webbs wanted a house that was on a par with the
mansions of Newport. The Queen Anne-style structure they
designed, with its brick siding, clustered chimneys, peak-roofed dormers, and turrets, had more than 100 rooms and
was the largest in Vermont when it was completed in 1899.

But what I like about the inn is that everything remains
as it was when the Webbs lived here. You can sit in the li-

brary on a luxurious low couch and page through a book from their collection. Tea is served every day at 3:30. A classic old pool table still stands in the game room, surrounded by sporting trophies from around the world. You dine in the opulent Marble Dining Room, where the food and the service are magnificent.

Best of all, each bedroom is furnished approximately as the Webbs left it. I am writing this on my seventh wedding anniversary, at Lila Webb's desk, which looks like a white baby grand piano. Its drawers and compartments are lined with blue velvet. Each piece of furniture in the room is a treasure — the large pink canopy bed, the low-slung overstuffed chair, the two walnut armoires, the marble-topped table with gilded legs, the white ceramic-tile fireplace and mantel — but the room as a whole is a jumble. Lila's desk is positioned in a turret in a corner of the room. I can look out and see the cove, where the Webbs once docked their 117-foot yacht, and the Coach Barn, where they kept their collection of more than 80 carriages. To my left are Lila's formal English flower gardens, glowing in the light of the late-afternoon sun setting over Lake Champlain and the Adirondack Mountains. A couple are wandering through the gardens, admiring the flowers and statuary. No doubt they feel as I do, happy to be houseguests of the Webbs.

Laura and I don't leave Shelburne Farms when we're staying at the inn. Our car goes unused for days. We avoid all modern interruptions to our 19th-century reverie. A friend who stayed at the inn recently was surprised that I am such a fan. She thought it was too luxurious for my taste, and in many regards it is. Though I find them curious, I can do without the excesses of the Webbs. Instead, my wife and I return to the inn for a different sort of luxury: the luxury of living in another time, when life was slower and — for the very rich, at least — carefree.

– Jamie Trowbridge

Editors' Picks for Vermont Romantic Retreats

General Information

Lake Champlain Regional Chamber of Commerce, 60 Main St., Suite 100, Burlington, VT 05401. 802-863-3489. (www.vermont.org)

For more information on Burlington, don't miss "Listening to Lake Champlain" on page 77.

Where to Stay

The Inn at Shelburne Farms, 1611 Harbor Rd., Shelburne, VT 05482. 802-985-8498. (Located seven miles southwest of Burlington, off Rte. 7.) The mansion, built on a 1,400-acre estate that overlooks Lake Champlain, offers two cottages, plus 24 guest rooms, 17 with private baths, and walking trails, swimming, tennis, and boating. Weekend guests must stay two nights. Open mid-May to mid-October. Afternoon tea, access to hiking trails, and free tours of the farm included. $100-$350. Restaurant open daily to nonguests for breakfast, dinner, and Sunday brunch. Reservations for both inn and restaurant should be made far in advance. $$$-$$$$.

Other Vermont Romantic Retreats

Windham Hill Inn, 311 Lawrence Dr., West Townshend, VT 05359. 800-944-4080, 802-874-4080. The inn is a converted farmhouse that offers 21 rooms, all with private baths, many with fireplaces, soaking tubs, or Jacuzzis. Located high on a hill at the end of a country road, guests here say that when they walk through the door, they feel a million miles away. The most romantic room is Meadowlook, a loft room in a newly converted barn. It is one of the largest rooms and has a soaking tub in front of the fireplace, double shower, and balcony with a superb view. Chef Cameron Howard works magic in the kitchen. The cuisine, called "refined French country" by *The Boston Globe*, shows off her talent for tasty and innovative sauces. Open year-round. Breakfast, dinner for two, and gratuity included. $245-$420. (www.windhamhill.com)

Inn at Ormsby Hill, Rte. 7A, 1842 Main St., Manchester Center, VT 05255. 800-670-2841, 802-362-1163. You will find everything you want in this fully restored circa 1764 manor home. Luxurious rooms are beautifully appointed, all have fireplaces and Jacuzzis, and most have canopy beds (all queen- or king-size). The dining room, where guests enjoy gourmet breakfasts (the inn's signature meal), has a spectacular set of windows looking out on the Green Mountains. On Friday nights guests have the option of "eating in." A delicious homemade dinner, for example baked four-cheese pasta with sausage or lemon chicken, is served to guests for an additional charge of $30. One of the most romantic rooms is the Tower Room, a second- and third-floor room with a 360-degree view of the mountains. The room has a queen-size tiger maple bow-topped canopy bed with fireplace sitting area, lots of windows, Jacuzzi for two, and double steam shower. Open year-round. Breakfast included. $160-$290. (www.ormsbyhill.com)

Rabbit Hill Inn, Rte. 18, Lower Waterford, VT 05848. 800-762-8669 (76 B-U-N-N-Y). Couples have followed their hearts to this lovely inn nestled between the Connecticut River and the White Mountains since 1795, when it was built as a traveler's lodge. Here you will find 21 guest rooms, all with private baths, most with fireplaces, some with private porches, each room with its own themed decor. One of the most romantic rooms, the Nest, is a suite with a queen-size canopy bed facing the fire, large dressing room with whirlpool for two, and private sunporch. A team of chefs prepares fantastic New American cuisine. Open year-round, except early November and late March. Full gourmet breakfast, dinner, afternoon tea, and pastry included. $210-$350. (www.rabbithillinn.com)

Cornucopia of Dorset, Rte. 30, P.O. Box 307, Dorset, VT 05251. 800-566-5751, 802-867-5751. You can't get more idyllic than the setting for this 19th-century Colonial home, which is located near the handsome green in Dorset, one of Vermont's prettiest towns. Five deluxe rooms are named for local mountains, all have private baths and four-poster or canopy beds, and four have fireplaces. Guests are greeted with champagne, and all the rooms have fresh fruit, chocolates, and homemade cookies. One of the most romantic rooms is the cottage suite, Owl's Head. Here you will find a loft bedroom with skylights overlooking the living room with cathedral ceiling, a wood-burning fireplace, large bath, private patio, and fully equipped kitchen. Open year-round, except April. Full candlelit breakfast and afternoon refreshments included. $125-$175, cottage $210-$245. (www.cornucopiaofdorset.com)

Listening to Lake Champlain

WE LISTEN TO WHAT LAKE CHAMPLAIN AND THE weather tell us. Burlington sits on a hillside that rises up from the waterfront like the inside of a shallow bowl. All winter long, with the leaves down from the trees, we watch the lake, freezing late in January then thawing in March, windswept and white-capped, occasionally calming down into a mirror that reflects New York's Adirondacks on the far side.

As the weather warms, our truest impulse, as inevitable as gravity, is to head downhill toward that balmy scent of warming lake water. Ninety-five feet above sea level, Lake Champlain is the lowest point in Vermont. After supper one evening in early May, my wife and daughters and I will take a notion to head down to the lake. Suddenly exuberant, we'll leave our dishes on the table and forget our jackets and sweaters. It's warm enough without them. What we want, without quite knowing why, is to stand near the shore and look out across that shimmering surface.

Recently the best place to go has become the Community Boathouse, a public facility with the aura of an old-fashioned private club. It's a double-decked, permanently anchored barge with a function room upstairs and walk-around decks top and bottom, a place for parties and poetry readings and jazz jam sessions, a place to walk and sit and contemplate the remaining beauty of the planet. At the boathouse bulletin board, we don't sign up for "Stories by

The Burlington Community Boathouse offers boat rentals, sailing lessons, and fishing charters on Lake Champlain. (photo by Carolyn Bates, courtesy Lake Champlain Regional Chamber of Commerce)

Wolfsong" or "Yoga by the Lake" or a sailing lesson, but we say maybe we'll take a cruise sometime soon.

Waterfront Park and the promenade invites us to take a little stroll in the day's last light, to chat on the boardwalk with our neighbors, check out the cyclists and skaters cruising the bike path, nod in passing to this spring's bench-sitting lovers and senior citizens. Lindsey, Bess, Molly, and I lean against the overlook railing to let the sunset have its way with our mood. Then we get right down there on the rocks and practice skimming flat pebbles across the water.

When the light's gone but it's not quite time to head home, we'll go to Church Street with its sidewalk cafés and street musicians. The air is warmer up here; it smells like pizza. It has been months since we walked downtown like this. To celebrate, we make our way toward Ben & Jerry's, where even among the out-of-towners we'll see people we know, and where the world's most sinful ice cream is handed to us by notably jovial scoopers. My wife and I go for the mixed-on-the-spot raspberry yogurt. My youngest likes the chocolate chip cookie dough sundae; my oldest has the sampler of raspberry, lemon, and mandarin orange ices. If we're lucky, we get one of the three window booths.

When our cups have been scraped clean, we turn toward home. Simple as that, we haul ourselves up the hill, yawning and teasing, maybe even quarreling in our cheerful, familial way. It's an easy hand-holding walk home. Moving up Pearl Street beneath streetlights and shadows, we savor what's up there ahead of us, our house and bedtime and all the rest of spring, not to mention summer coming.

– *David Huddle*

Editors' Picks for Burlington

General Information

The Lake Champlain Regional Chamber of Commerce Burlington Convention and Visitors Bureau, 60 Main St., Suite 100, Burlington, VT 05401. 802-863-3489. (www.vermont.org)

Community Boathouse, College St., Burlington, VT 05401. 802-865-3377. Open 24 hours a day starting May 15.

Where to Stay

Radisson Hotel Burlington, 60 Battery St., Burlington, VT 05401. 800-333-3333, 802-658-6500. Location, location, location: This fine hotel overlooks lovely Lake Champlain and the Adirondack Mountains — a big-city hotel with all the amenities, within walking distance to the waterfront and downtown. Open year-round. $109-$199. Oak Street Café open daily for breakfast, lunch, and dinner; $-$$. Seasons on the Lake open Tuesday-Saturday for dinner; $$. (www.radisson.com/burlingtonvt)

Willard Street Inn, 349 Willard St., Burlington, VT 05401. 800-577-8712, 802-651-8710. This stately Victorian was built in 1881 by a prominent banker on what is now the main thoroughfare through lively downtown. It served as a private home for 100 years and was finally opened as an inn in 1996 after a thorough renovation. Ten of the 15 rooms have private baths and some have views of Lake Champlain. Open year-round. Breakfast and afternoon tea included. $80-$200. (www.willardstreetinn.com)

Thomas Mott Bed & Breakfast, Blue Rock Rd. on Lake Champlain, Alburg, VT 05440. 800-348-0843. This completely restored 1838 farmhouse overlooks Lake Champlain, the Adirondacks, Jay Peak, and Mount Mansfield. Amenities at the five-room B&B include a game room, quilts, ceiling fans, a gazebo, canoes, fishing, and a private dock extending onto the lake. All rooms with private bath. Oh yes, and complimentary Ben & Jerry's ice cream! Open year-round. Full breakfast included. $75-$95. (www.thomas-mott-bb.com)

Where to Eat

Ben & Jerry's, 30 Community Dr., South Burlington. 802-651-9600. The original site of these now-famous gourmet scoops.

Perry's Fish House, Rte. 7, 1080 Shelburne Rd., South Burlington. 802-862-1300. When you see the large, carved wooden lobster and the old boat outside a weathered building, you've arrived at Perry's. Chosen the best seafood restaurant in the area each year from 1993 to 1997 by the *Burlington Free Press* readers' poll, this is a large, festive eatery. The restaurant is definitely kid-friendly; they even get crayons. Landlubbers can choose chicken, prime rib, or steak. Open Monday-Thursday 5-10 P.M., Friday-Saturday 4:30-11 P.M., Sunday 4-10 P.M. $$-$$$.

The Blue Seal Restaurant, Bridge St., Richmond. 802-434-5949. When diners are willing to drive up to an hour and a half round-trip in the Vermont winter, you know the meals must be special. From its Caesar salad with roasted peppers to its pan-roasted salmon, this is a restaurant where fresh produce and innovation matter. Situated in a granary built in 1854 in downtown Richmond, it's the perfect spot for a romantic, leisurely evening. Open Tuesday-Saturday 5:30-9:30 P.M. for dinner (Sunday, too, during foliage season). $$.

The Cheese Outlet and Fresh Market, 400 Pine St., Burlington. 802-863-3968. For 20 years this has been the prime spot for gourmet shopping. Cheeses, pâtés, imported olives; imported wines and microbrewery beers; breads and rolls; cookies, scones, and homemade pies; ready-made salads and sandwiches; fresh fruit; and more. The Vermont-made Blue Moon sorbet alone in flavors like mango passion and grapefruit Campari makes this worth a visit. Open daily 8-7, Sunday 10-5. $.

What to See

Lake Champlain Maritime Museum at Basin Harbor, 4472 Basin Harbor Rd., Vergennes. 802-475-2022. Here you'll discover why Lake Champlain is considered the most historic body of water in North America. Explore the vibrant history and characters of the Champlain Valley through its military, commercial, and regional periods. Climb aboard the 54-foot replica gunboat *Philadelphia II* and step back in time. Open mid-May to mid-October 10-5. $7, seniors $6, children 6-15 $3, children under 6 and museum members free. (www.lcmm.org)

Lake Champlain Basin Science Center, 1 College St., Burlington. 802-864-1848. The science center features three exhibits: "Secrets of the Lake," "The Sea That Used to Be," and "Buzz, Croak & Warble: Song of the Wetlands" — live turtles, snakes, frogs, and fish, demonstrations, hands-on interactives, including microscopes and a turtle tank. Open in summer daily 11-5. $2, children 2-12 $1. (www.uvm.edu/~lcbsc)

The Spirit of Ethan Allen II, Burlington Boathouse, College St., Burlington. 802-862-8300. See the lake aboard the *Spirit of Ethan Allen II,* a 500-passenger triple-deck cruise ship. Narrated scenic cruises depart daily, and there are special lunch, brunch, and dinner cruises. Sails May-October. Prices vary.

A Writer's Retreat on the Shores of Caspian Lake

SUMMER HAS GONE FROM CASPIAN LAKE. *LABOR* Day has taken the first of the vacationing crowd back to teaching posts at Princeton and Harvard and Yale. Come mid-October the town crew will close off the waterline to the camps on Caspian, boards will be nailed over windows, and the last of the "shoulder people" (those who stay past the traditional Labor Day exodus) will be shaken from the lake's shore like sand from a rug. The summer population of 2,000 will shrink to the 717 year-rounders. It will be, as summer resident Wallace Stegner once wrote, "as if a large room were suddenly emptied of people, and those who were left hitched their chairs in a closer, more intimate, more self-sufficient circle around the fire."

Those who stay say they know it's fall when they finally have their pick of parking spots at the crossroads in front of Willey's Store. They have their pick of books at the Greensboro Free Library, where the shelves have been bare all summer. Dan Cohen, the town's librarian, has closed the door against the cold that can bring snow in October to this northern Vermont town. Through it, he hears the first shots of deer season and sees the shadows lengthen across the rows of books in the "Greensboro Authors" section. No other town this size, set so far from a two-lane highway, could boast such a show of talent as this: Close to 200 authors have lived or summered here. Those who have taken inspiration

Highland Lodge is a cozy Victorian-era inn that offers swimming and boating on Caspian Lake in summer and Nordic skiing in winter. (courtesy Highland Lodge)

from the glacially carved landscape include Supreme Court Chief Justice William Rehnquist, "Ask Beth" columnist Beth Winship, Pulitzer Prize-winner Wallace Stegner, anthropologist Margaret Mead, runner/writer James Fixx, and journalist John Gunther.

One of the first of the writers to discover this haven on the western corner of the Northeast Kingdom was Bliss Perry, a Princeton scholar who brought his family to Caspian Lake in 1897. He later wrote in his autobiography: "We had marvelous air, and in that high altitude, restful scenery, absolute quiet; it was the unspoiled essence of primitive Vermont. The lake was perfect for bathing and boating. There were big 'squaretails' in it then, and plenty of landlocked salmon and 'lakers' . . ."

When he returned to campus that fall, he told his colleagues. The following summer the Perrys had company at the lake. And the next year the number of spectacled scholars mixed in with the local farmers and mechanics at the general-store checkout grew. When Perry later worked at Harvard and Williams and at *The Atlantic Monthly*, word about the summer colony of writers in Greensboro spread even further.

More embarked upon the lengthy train ride from New York or Connecticut or Boston to the station in Greensboro Bend. A buggy took them the final four miles from there, and when they crested the last hill, they saw before them the long view of Caspian Lake. Over the long summer holidays, there was time enough to acquaint themselves with local customs and to build cottages (called "camps" locally) and "think houses" on the seven miles of Caspian's shoreline. They settled in clusters that took on the flavor of neighborhoods — Aspenhurst and Winnimere — each with its own summer traditions. They listened from canoes to classical music broadcast over the waters on Sunday evenings, played golf in a pasture with, at first, only three tomato cans for holes, enjoyed picnics on Barr Hill with a view sweeping down rolling farmland to the mile-long lake.

There was time enough for both recreation and the creation of books. In fact, so many academics found favor with Greensboro that one summer an editor asked a history professor, "Do all historians go to Greensboro, Vermont, in the summer?" The editor had three whose addresses were simply: Greensboro, VT 05841. In reply, history professor Allen Davis wrote, "To those of us who combine writing with pleasure, there is no better address."

He and the others set their typewriters toward the views or scribbled notes in the shade of trees clumped at the water's edge. Works took shape in almost every form imaginable: scientific treatises on molecular biology, histories of 17th-century Asian philosophers, mathematics textbooks, cookbooks, collections of sermons and poetry, Harlequin romances, books on spiritual dowsing. Cedric Whitman, a Harvard classicist and poet, wrote large parts of his books on Sophocles and Homer in the upstairs room of the old library. Wallace Stegner set two of his novels — *Second Growth* and *Crossing to Safety* — in fictionalized versions of Greensboro.

Though he spent most of the year out west, Stegner looked forward to his time in Vermont. In the foreword to the town's bicentennial history in 1990, he wrote: "From the first day I saw it, I responded to Greensboro because it had what I lacked and wanted: permanence, tranquillity, traditional and customary acceptances, a stable and neighborly social order. I envied people like Lewis Hill their ancestry and the sureness with which they knew who they were and where they belonged."

Lewis Hill lives with his wife, Nancy, who is also a writer, in a white hilltop house that has belonged to his family since 1812. Another author, Krissie Ohlrogge, had been a Caspian Lake summer kid who dreamed at age 14 of someday staying on year-round at her family's farmstead to write and have babies. In her early twenties she made the move back to Greensboro and through the long, cold winter wrote her first romance. It sold. In the two decades since, she has

WHAT THE
LOCALS
KNOW

Best Shopping: From Woolens to Daylilies

The little town of Greensboro offers terrific shopping — the kind worth driving out of your way for. Right downtown, don't miss Willey's, one of the best general stores in New England. Right across the street the Miller's Thumb sells high-quality crafts, Portuguese ceramics, and April Cornell clothing. Old Forge Scottish Woollens, a shop in the Lakeview Inn, has the nicest sweaters we've seen anywhere. (Don't think we've spelled woolens wrong here; this is the real way, we're told by shopkeeper Karen Coburn.) Just 1½ miles out of town on Barr Hill Road you'll find daylily heaven. Andrea Perham and her husband, Dave, run Vermont Daylilies, where you can find over 400 different kinds of daylilies to admire and buy. From mid-July to mid-August the field across from their house is in full bloom. Picture assorted colors of daylilies, mature clumps of each, of 400 varieties!

Willey's, Main St. 802-533-2621. Open weekdays 7-5:30, weekends 8-5:30.

The Miller's Thumb, 4 Main St. 802-533-2960. Open daily 9-6, shorter hours in winter.

Old Forge Scottish Woollens, in the Lakeview Inn, Main St. 802-533-2241. Open daily 10-5.

Vermont Daylilies, Barr Hill Rd. 802-533-7155. Open July 1-Labor Day Wednesday-Sunday noon-5.

The Woodstock Garden Club visits Vermont Daylilies. (courtesy Vermont Daylilies)

written more than 40 more for several publishers, under her pen name, Anne Stuart.

Krissie's friend and neighbor Bridget Collier works from Monday to Thursday as the town clerk. She devotes Fridays to writing. She wrote her first book in 1978 during a two-week vacation. By the second week she was out of money, so she wrote for 12-hour days and at the end of the week had finished a Western. Her mother, Leona Collier, the former town librarian author of two Regency romances, typed the manuscript for her, and it was published. Since then, Bridget has written five more Westerns and is currently writing a book on coping with Alzheimer's. "Growing up in a town like this, with so many writers around," she says, "I just didn't think twice about writing."

The time in summer when most writers come out of hiding is the hour when *The New York Times* and *The Boston Globe* are delivered to the general store. Willey's sells more than 200 of the out-of-town dailies then. But following Columbus Day, talk of those faraway places fades as surely as the leaves settle to the ground. Willey's discontinues the big-city papers. During the cold months, the year-rounders will content themselves with news closer to home. Words from Hardwick and St. Johnsbury and Montpelier will be enough to keep them warm for the coming cold season in Greensboro.

– Christine Schultz

Editors' Picks for Greensboro, Craftsbury, and St. Johnsbury

General Information

Directions: Take Interstate 91 north to St. Johnsbury, exit onto Rte. 2 west, then right on Rte. 15 in West Danville. Turn north onto Rte. 16, 2 miles to East Hardwick. There, turn west and follow the signs; at the first four-corners turn right, 2 miles to Greensboro.

State of Vermont Department of Tourism and Marketing, Travel Information, 134 State St., Montpelier, VT 05602. 802-828-3237. For a travel packet call 800-837-6668 (V-E-R-M-O-N-T). Travel tip: peak foliage color generally hits Greensboro the last week in September or the first week in October. Make reservations early, since inns across the state fill up fast at this time. For twice-weekly foliage and seasonal updates call the Vermont information hot line, 802-828-3239. (www.travel-vermont.com)

Northeast Kingdom Chamber of Commerce, 30 Western Ave., St. Johnsbury, VT 05819. 800-639-6379 or 802-748-3678. Stop in at its year-round walk-in office, or check out its seasonal information booth at the corner of Main St. and Eastern Ave. (www.vermontNEKchamber.org)

Where to Stay and Eat (Well)

The Highland Lodge, Caspian Lake Rd., Greensboro, VT 05841. 802-533-2647. Run by David and Wilhelmina Smith, the lodge offers 11 rooms, some with a view of the lake, and 11 cottages. Swimming, canoeing, sailing, tennis, 120 acres of woodlands and fields, and a playhouse with scheduled activities for children. Open May 25-October 15; December 23-March 15. Full breakfast, dinner, and gratuity included. Single $100-$145, couple $179-$240. Restaurant open for breakfast, lunch, and dinner. Delicious, imaginative food prepared with Vermont products. (The Smiths are part of the Vermont Fresh Network, an organization that coordinates farmers with restaurants for use of local products.) $$-$$$. (www.pbpub.com/vermont/hiland.htm)

Lakeview Inn, Main St., P.O. Box 180, Greensboro, VT 05841. 802-533-2291. Owned and operated by the Hunt family, this bed-and-breakfast inn has 12 rooms with private baths. The circa 1872 Victorian Italianate building with sweeping veranda has recently been restored according to historic-preservation guidelines. Open year-round. Breakfast included. $80-$115. Café and bakery serving home-made breads, gourmet deli sandwiches, fresh fruit tarts. Open daily 7-7. $.

Inn on the Common, Main St., Craftsbury Common, VT 05827. 800-521-2233, 802-586-9619. This handsome Federal-style building is one of the oldest in the county. It has 16 individually decorated rooms with private baths, some with fireplaces, stoves, and canopy beds. Swimming pool in summer, outdoor tennis court, beautiful perennial garden. Award-winning wine list. You won't find fancier lodging in northeast Vermont. Open year-round. Full breakfast and five-course dinner included. $230-$290. Also serves fixed-price dinner for $40. (www.innonthecommon.com)

New Hampshire

Hancock Covered Bridge (photo by David Voorhis)

It's Never Lonely at the Top

The World's Most Climbed Mountain: Monadnock

When we behold this summit at this season of the year far away and blue in the horizon, we may think of the blueberries as blending their color with the general blueness of the mountain.
— HENRY DAVID THOREAU

THOSE WHO FIRST CLIMBED MOUNT MONADNOCK for fun in the early 1800s probably went in search of those blueberries of which Thoreau wrote. Hikers today can still scale Monadnock's slopes and return with buckets brimming with berries. There may be easier places to find that azure fruit, but perhaps none so scenic as Monadnock. When you pause there in your picking to sample the harvest, you see below you New Hampshire's kingdom, and the burst of berry that moistens your mouth is somehow made sweeter.

Blueberries, though, are certainly not the mountain's only attraction. Mount Monadnock's reputation has risen higher than its elevation, but that doesn't stop southern New Hampshire from championing it as the region's claim to fame. And with good reason. Monadnock is considered the most climbed mountain in the world. (Until a few years ago, Mount Fuji had that distinction. But since the Japanese built a road to within a few hundred feet of the top, there's not much "climbing" necessary. It is still the world's most summited mountain, however!)

Its name, "the mountain that stands alone," has inspired a geological term. Numerous writers, such as Thoreau, Emerson, and Whittier, have rhapsodized over its beauty, and painters have coated enough canvas with the humpback form to build a tent big enough to cover it. Furthermore, the bare-topped Monadnock ranks as one of only 13 mountains listed in the National Register of Natural Landmarks. Its summit contains alpine vegetation similar to that on Mount Washington, which is twice as high. And Monadnock's summit is the only place where you can see all six New England states at one time, more than 100 miles in any direction.

Even given that, who'd have guessed that a 3,165-foot peak could draw so much attention to itself? But each year more than 125,000 people make the trek to the bare, rocky summit. Many come because it's so accessible (located just 65 miles northwest of Boston), so high above everything around it, yet so low that almost anyone can climb it.

Most come at the same time and most travel the same trails. Mike Walsh, Monadnock State Park manager, estimates that five percent of each year's climbers come on the same day. The swell starts with the foliage flush the last weekend in September and the first in October. On Columbus Day weekend more than 6,000 people set out in search of Monadnock's summit, making it the second-most populous place in Cheshire County — for a day.

"Our mountain is a comfortable little mountain," Newton F. Tolman from nearby Nelson wrote in *North of Monadnock*, "in spite of the impassioned attempts by so many New England writers to endow it with the awesome majesty of an alp." He's right. Monadnock is the people's mountain, and with a choice of six trailheads to start from and 36 maintained trails (totaling 40 miles), there's something for everyone. If you ask, the park rangers (a friendly bunch) will give you a map of the less-crowded trails.

Anyone in reasonably good shape and well-equipped can make the climb. Wear stiff sneakers or hiking boots, and carry food, water, and a warm sweater for the summit. Make

Each year more than 125,000 people climb Mount Monadnock. From its rocky summit on clear day hikers can see the Boston skyline. (photo by Carole Allen)

Best Berries

It is summer, the season of dog days and lemonade afternoons, and there isn't a cloud in the sky. You are standing at the head of a gentle green hill before countless rows of blueberry bushes heavy with ripe fruit. Behind these, Mount Monadnock rises in the distance. Bucket in hand, you enjoy a morning of premier picking, and find raspberries, blueberry plants, cold drinks, local produce, baked goods, and goats for petting, too. There's even a sandbox for young pickers who run out of steam. Though wild blueberries sing like no other fruit, the varieties cultivated here are the tastiest we've found. Fingertips and tongues may be blue, but your spirit will be just the opposite. Open daily about mid-July to mid-October (depending on the ripeness of the berries, so call ahead), 8 A.M.-dusk. (Price per pound varies weekly.)

Monadnock Berries, 545 West Hill Rd., Troy (follow signs from the common). 603-242-6417.

it easier on the next to come and on the rangers (who pack out an estimated 500 pounds of garbage each year) by taking all you have brought in back out with you.

The shortest way to go (and one of the most popular routes) is the White Dot Trail. It leaves from the park headquarters and makes a direct line to the top in 1.9 steep miles. William Royce laid out the trail in 1900 and is said to have ridden his horse to the summit on this trail. But no horses (or dogs) are allowed on the mountain these days — you'll have to go by foot. Better allow three to four hours round-trip for the climb.

If you're not set on reaching the summit, try the Cliff Walk Trail (about two miles long via the Lost Farm Trail from park headquarters). It offers a gradual climb that opens unexpectedly from thick woods onto Point Surprise, a rock outcropping with a spectacular view to the south and east. You'll pass Thoreau's Seat, Emerson's Seat (Ralph Waldo Emerson's favorite spot), the Old Graphite Mine, and the Wolf Dens. Though wolves did once live beneath fallen spruce on the mountaintop, farmers, frustrated at losing so many sheep, set fire to the peak in the 1820s, burned out the wolves, and denuded the summit for good. Allow four hours round-trip.

The White Arrow Trail on the south side is perhaps the mountain's oldest trail (set in 1706). It is wide and well worn, though rocky, and climbs steeply at times through yellow birch and spruce woods. You'll pass over wide stone steps laid by the U.S. Geodetic Survey crews in 1861. "Emerson used to stroll up the south side dressed as though he were walking up Beacon Street," a local writer noted. Several turn-of-the-century photographs show ladies in long dresses picnicking under parasols on the summit, but you may find your hike less of an elegant occasion. Be prepared to sweat.

If you'd like to see what you and the mountain are made of, the steepest section of trail — 700 feet in half a mile — lies on the Spellman Trail. Despite the steep ascent, it's not a difficult climb, the guidebook assures you. The spectacular views to the east may make it worth the workout. The Spellman Trail joins the Cascade Link to the Pumpelly Trail, making it a 2.9-mile hike in all from park headquarters to the summit.

"They who simply climb to the peak of Monadnock have seen but little of the mountain," Thoreau wrote in his journal. "I came not to look off from it, but to look at it. The view of the pinnacle itself from the plateau below surpasses any view which you get from the summit." One of the best places to admire the view is at the aptly named Inspiration Rock. (Since no official trail exists to get you there, it would be wise to ask for specific "bushwhacking" instructions from the park staff.) At 2,660 feet, just south of the White Cross Trail, you'll see a remarkable silhouette of the summit and marvelous views to the east down Mead's Brook ravine.

If you're not determined to get to the summit or if you have children along, there are other options. You can camp at the base, where 21 family sites are available year-round (half on a first-come, first-served basis; the other half reservable), and explore the Monadnock Garden Club's trail within a short walk of park headquarters. There you'll find some 400 species of wildflowers — turtleheads, arrowheads, asters — and 50 fern varieties.

Those who settled the area saw immediately how distracting the mountain's beauty could be and took the necessary precautions. "Our ancestors who cleared the farms were an austere, pious breed," Tolman wrote. "They took no chances. Wherever a house had a fine outlook, invariably a huge barn was built squarely in front of it. Plainly, the builders figured the going would be hard enough in this stony wilderness without their womenfolk getting starry-eyed from gazing at Monadnock."

– Christine Schultz

Editors' Picks for the Monadnock Region

General Information

Monadnock Travel Council, P.O. Box 358, Keene, NH 03431. 800-432-7864, 603-352-1303.

Monadnock State Park, P.O. Box 181, Jaffrey, NH 03452. 603-532-8862. (To reserve a base campsite for your family or youth group: 603-271-3628.) The park headquarters is located off Rte. 124, four miles west of Jaffrey. Pets are not permitted. Open year-round. $2.50 per person; N.H. seniors and all children under 12 free; group rates available (call ahead).

Where to Stay

Woodbound Inn, Woodbound Rd., Rindge, NH 03461. 800-688-7770, 603-532-8341. This rambling inn on Lake Contoocook offers views of Mount Monadnock from the nine-hole golf course and sandy beach. Stay in lakefront cabins with fireplaces or more modern rooms in the main inn, which has 25 rooms (14 with private baths; two hall baths available to the other rooms). Open year-round. Breakfast included. $89-$199. Open Tuesday-Saturday for dinner. $$-$$$. (www.nhweb.com/woodbound/Index.html)

Inn at East Hill Farm, 460 Monadnock St., Troy, NH 03465. 603-242-6495. This farm resort is nothin' fancy but offers the whole family plenty to do. Facilities and activities included in price: indoor and outdoor pools and whirlpools, sauna, lake beach, tennis court, shuffleboard, working farm, boats, fishing, waterskiing (late June-August), and square dancing. Horseback riding is available for an additional fee. Set on a back road south of Mount Monadnock, this inn provides a view of the summit just over the pond. Stay in cottages, inn rooms, or suites sprinkled over 150 acres. Open year-round. Three meals daily included. $70-$88; children $58-$68; ages 2-4 $25-$35; under 2 free. (www.east-hill-farm.com)

Where to Eat

Tolman's Table, Center at Keene, 149 Emerald St., Keene. 603-355-8923. This gem is located in a strip mall, but once you step inside, the murals of pasture and barnyard animals transport you to a country farmhouse. Sit down to one of Scot's tasty dishes, such as Yankee pot roast or meatloaf, and join his efforts to preserve the "family dinner." (By the way, that's his mom and dad serving you.) Open Tuesday-Friday for lunch, Tuesday-Saturday for dinner. $$.

Monadnock Mountain View Restaurant, Village Gathering Mall, Rte. 12, Troy. 603-242-3300. You won't find any gourmet flourishes on the menu, because this restaurant doesn't need fancy food to impress — it seasons every meal with a view of Mount Monadnock that is the best of any eatery in the region. You'll always get a good meal and courteous service. Open Monday-Saturday for lunch, Wednesday-Saturday for dinner; Sunday 9:30-1 for brunch, 11-7 for dinner. $-$$.

Gap Mountain Breads, Rte. 12 on the common, Troy. 603-242-3284. In the morning, come early to snag a warm cinnamon bun. For lunch or dinner, try homemade soups, sandwiches, and pizzas. Never leave without a loaf of fresh bread or a bag of cookies. Open Monday-Tuesday 8-5, Wednesday-Thursday 8-8, Friday-Saturday 8 A.M.-9 P.M. $.

Wolfeboro: Winnipesaukee's First Resort

WOLFEBORO CALLS ITSELF "THE OLDEST SUMMER RESORT in America," which, we suppose, makes Colonial governor John Wentworth the first of the summer people. Wentworth erected an oversize cottage on a nearby lake in 1763, and by the time his manse burned down in 1820, Wolfeboro was ensconced as a seasonal getaway.

What drew the rusticators then, and draws them still, is a body of water as big as its name, Lake Winnipesaukee. Abenaki for "lake in a high place," "Winnipesaukee" is a Native American real-estate claim that holds up to the

severest scrutiny. Pine-topped knolls of the White Mountain foothills ring Winnipesaukee's lobes, creating an alpine-
lake environment where summer is as sweet as the wild
blackberries of August.

Lulled by the faint buzz of small powerboats,
Wolfeboro surveys the east end of the lake from the mouth
of a protected bay, announcing itself to the water approach
with a terse sign on the roof of P. J.'s Dockside: "Wolfeboro.
Established 1770. Population 4,807." Steam locomotives
used to bring passengers right to the docks to board cruising
steamships. Now you'll drive in on Route 28, traversing the
rolling countryside. At the bottom of a hill you'll land in
Wolfeboro's compact center, a lakeside rim of pastel and
brick buildings housing souvenir shops, sporting-goods re-
tailers, restaurants, and ice-cream stands.

Wolfeboro's charm is evident in a glance: the lake, the
woodsy shore, the genial country architecture, and the
promise of indolence induced by warm sun, tranquil views,
and an unhurried pace. A turn-of-the-century postcard in
the historical society could have been written last week: *"This
is a pretty place but decidedly quiet. Wish you and Mabel were
here. We play 'Bridge' and I am trying to learn to swim. Old dogs,
new tricks. – Nell"*

Today Nell might branch out to include deepwater
diving or lakeshore kayaking to augment the basic, do-little
vacation that has never gone out of style in Wolfeboro. But
hardly anything of consequence has changed since Nell's
day, calling to mind the Yankee nostrum of not fixing what
isn't broken.

The docks are the nerve center of the town — home to
a smattering of casual restaurants, a tiny waterside park,
stops for the trolley and tour buses. Just behind the picnic tables of the venerable P. J.'s Dockside restaurant, the largest
town landing reaches out into the lake. On a regular schedule, a great blast from the horn of M/S *Mount Washington*
startles those on the dock. But don't set your watch by this
announcement of a forthcoming cruise. Time (especially

summer time) is an elastic commodity in Wolfeboro. The behemoth vessel — first built for service on Lake Champlain in 1888, moved to Winnipesaukee in 1940, and cut apart and expanded in 1982 — shuttles between honky-tonk Weirs Beach and sedate Wolfeboro, crossing and recrossing the lake. What use is punctuality? The point is not to arrive but to be in motion, passing many of the 365 islands on the lake's 72 square miles, scanning the coast to ogle the private compounds of the summer people.

The M/S Mount Washington, *a New Hampshire landmark, cruises the beautiful waters of Lake Winnipesaukee.* (*courtesy Mount Washington Cruises*)

From Winnipesaukee's 186 miles of mainland shore, Wolfeboro claims two small public beaches and another on nearby Lake Wentworth. Winnipesaukee's lake beaches are remarkable for their sheer simplicity: a parking lot, sand, warm water that gently tapers to diving depth, bathhouses at some, a lifeguard stand, a float anchored in a roped-off swimming area. Each beach recedes to a stand of red pines that provides shady respite from the midday sun. The light lap of water on sand punctuates the murmur of lazy conversation. If the weather cooperates, it's hard to imagine that anyone could ask more of summer — or of a summer place.

Wolfeboro plays into this languor, offering only enough mercantile activity to support vacationers with the staples. Black's Paper Store (depicted in the Main Street scene of Nell's postcard) remains the venue to pick up *The New York Times* or *The Boston Globe* as well as New Hampshire's *Union Leader*. Nearby, the Straw Cellar (a gift shop) offers a selection of souvenirs, many of them branded "Oldest Summer Resort in America." Hall's Pharmacy is a classic small-town American drugstore. Directly across Main Street stands a bench stenciled with the names of the threesome who claimed it as their own: Homer, George, and Henry.

The Country Bookseller on Railroad Avenue provides reading material to take to the beach or to a bench in the downtown's shady pocket park. Nor is there a shortage of sweets; favorites are the ice cream at both Bailey's Bubble and i scream on Railroad Avenue and the hand-dipped chocolates of Lee's Candy Kitchen on North Main Street.

Wolfeboro's museums, like its shops, are more diversions than destinations. The historical society cluster of three buildings staffed by volunteer guides provides a taste of Wolfeboro's past. The Clark House is a tidy example of country life in the early years of the Republic, and the adjacent schoolhouse exhibits some interesting bits and shards excavated from the cellar hole of the Governor Wentworth mansion. Antique fire-fighting equipment in gleaming condition fills a newer building on the grounds.

Wolfeboro's other museum addresses a past still in living memory. A half-mile scenic walk along Back Bay links the dockside downtown with Wolfeboro Falls, where the Wright Museum, devoted to the American experience from 1939 to 1945, opened in Wolfeboro in 1994. This museum blends a fascination with World War II vehicles (armored cars, a tank, an airplane) with the story of the home front, as told through posters, magazines, and reconstructed rooms. Clothing, furniture, appliances, and memorabilia still pour into the museum from local attics.

For a long time it seemed that only one fixture was missing from the otherwise complete resort-town scene. But the town remedied that in 1995, when it built a bandstand in the prime spot at the foot of Cate Park at the edge of the harbor. And they did it right. Only a dedicatory inscription discloses that this octagonal gazebo hasn't been around since the days of Queen Victoria. A string of performers appear throughout the summer — but the best night of all is Wednesday, when, during July and August, the Cate Park Band plays. "We welcome anyone with an instrument who happens to be in town," director Judy Robinson says cheerfully. "We rehearse at seven, and we sound just terrible."

She smiles and adds, "But we're perfect by the time the concert begins at eight."

– Patricia Harris and David Lyon

Editors' Picks for Wolfeboro

General Information

Wolfeboro Chamber of Commerce, 32 Central Ave., P.O. Box 547, Wolfeboro, NH 03894. 603-569-2200. (www.wolfeboro.com) The Web site is private but packed with events and travel information.

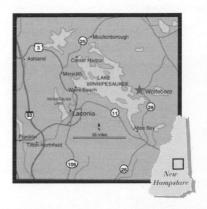

Where to Stay

The Lake Motel, Rte. 28, P.O. Box 887, Wolfeboro, NH 03894. 888-569-1110, 603-569-1100. A motel turned mini-resort on Crescent Lake between lakes Wentworth and Winnipesaukee. There are 29 rooms and five apartments. Open mid-May to mid-October. $73-$98 per couple; each additional person $6.

The Tuc' Me Inn, 118 North Main St., P.O. Box 657, Wolfeboro, NH 03894. 603-569-5702. There are seven rooms offered at this intimate 1850 B&B. Open year-round. All-you-can-eat country breakfast included. $75-$95.

The Wolfeboro Inn, 90 North Main St., P.O. Box 1270, Wolfeboro, NH 03894. 800-451-2389, 603-569-3016. Parts of the inn, the "fancy" place in town, date from 1812. Open year-round. Breakfast included. $79-$229. Wolfe's Tavern open daily for breakfast, lunch, and dinner, plus Sunday brunch; $-$$. The 1812 Room open daily for dinner; $$-$$$.

Where to Eat

P. J.'s Dockside, town docks, Wolfeboro. 603-569-6747. Family-oriented dockside dining spot with paneled walls and wooden booths. Open daily 7 A.M.-9 P.M. $-$$.

Wolfetrap, 19 Bay St., Wolfeboro. 603-569-1047. Bayfront view for raw bar and good seafood (famous for its lobster rolls). Open May-September (and possibly later, depending on fall weather). Open weekends noon-11; Monday-Friday 4-11 P.M. for dinner; restaurant's fish market (The Wolfe Catch) open daily 9-6. $$-$$$.

What to See

Molly the Trolley, Wolfeboro Trolley Company, town docks, Wolfeboro. 603-569-5257. Narrated 45-minute tours that start at the town docks but can be joined at any of the trolley's stopping points. Open July and August daily 10-4. All-day pass $3, children 4-12 $1, under 4 free.

M/S *Mount Washington,* daily departures from town docks. For schedules and prices call 603-366-2628.

Winnipesaukee Belle, town docks, Wolfeboro 603-569-3016. Hour-and-a-half cruises offered early July-early September, three times daily; early September to mid-October, two cruises daily. $10, children 4-12 $5, ages 3 and under free, Wolfeboro Inn guests free.

Wolfeboro Historical Society, South Main St., Wolfeboro. 603-569-4997. Open July-August Monday-Friday 11-4, Saturday 11-2. $3, students $2, children under 12 free.

Wright Museum of American Enterprise, 77 Center St., Wolfeboro. 603-569-1212. Open April-October daily 10-4; also open some winter weekends (call ahead); arrangements can be made throughout the year for museum to be opened for large group tours. $5, seniors and veterans $4, students $3, children under 8 free. (www.wrightmuseum.org)

A Foliage Cruise Along New Hampshire's Seacoast

WE KNEW WHAT IT WAS LIKE TO GLIMPSE FALL FO-
liage through a car window. We knew, too, the intimacy of an
autumn walk through the woods with the crunch of leaves
underfoot. That's why the notion of a third perspective so
beguiled us. On a foliage cruise with Portsmouth Harbor
Cruises, embarking from that New Hampshire seacoast
town for other points along the shore, we could get our color
twice over — in sharp, realist brush strokes on the shore and
in impressionist ones reflected in the water.

Walter Dunfey, skipper of the *Heritage*, carries a crew
of two: a first mate, who ladles out chowder from the galley,
and a salty Australian sheepdog named Matilda, who'll lap up
anything you don't. Dunfey chooses his route each afternoon

according to the prevailing tide and the wishes of his passengers. Often the *Heritage* will go up the Cocheco River toward Dover, where both the color and the quiet close in on you as the river narrows. We saw double-crested cormorants, Canada geese, and several great blue heron; we didn't see kingfishers, semipalmated plovers, snowy egrets, or on the shore, the occasional white-tailed deer, though. Every other year or so the *Heritage* encounters a bald eagle. Ospreys are the captain's favorite companions because they follow his boat upriver, plucking fish from the water in crowd-pleasing fashion. Dunfey has seen the Cocheco trip turn even the least likely bird-watcher into a confirmed Audubonite.

Sometimes the *Heritage*, heading up the Piscataqua River from Portsmouth, passes on the Cocheco and instead hangs a couple of lefts into Little Bay and then Great Bay, which is fringed by a National Wildlife Refuge. Great Bay is

Portsmouth Harbor Cruises offer great views of this port city that has seen 300 years of maritime industry.
(photo by James Lemass)

Prescott Park is famous for its lovely gardens. In the summer it is the location of Prescott Park Arts Festival performances. (courtesy Prescott Park Arts Festival)

an estuary, meaning both fresh and salt water intermingle, and our skipper showed us how the boat's wake gradually fades from a frothy white to something more crystalline as the water loses its salinity. We wound up seeing the changing of the colors in more ways than one.

The *Heritage* plies these routes during the summer, too, but by late September the seacoast's inland waterways have become a Romper Room for birds heading south. Harbor seals from the open sea also come here, both to enjoy the warmer water and to nurse shark bites suffered over the summer. Our captain subtitled all the sights with lore filtered through his whimsical and environmentalist sensibility. In the middle of Great Bay we learned the story of how local citizens kept Aristotle Onassis from building an oil refinery on its banks; the brief but fascinating history of New Franklin, New Hampshire, the state capital that never was; and several cautionary tales about buffalo farming.

Some 2½ hours later, returning to the hurly-burly of

Lo's Seafood & Oriental Market

Just inland from Portsmouth's charming waterfront is a different kind of sea: Woodbury Avenue is an ocean of strip malls, franchise eateries, and superstores. Good cooks brave the four lanes of traffic to shop at a small but excellent market called Lo's Seafood & Oriental Market. Inside, three aisles are crammed with imported foods and cookware, fresh Oriental produce, frozen delicacies, and the freshest fish in town. It has to be, because local Oriental families make sushi and other meals from the raw seafood sold here.

Lo's Seafood & Oriental Market, 1976 Woodbury Ave., Portsmouth. 603-431-0022.

Portsmouth Harbor, we regarded in a new light the twin piles of salt and scrap metal heaped high on the docks. The salt, brought by freighter from Chile to be dumped on New England's roads each winter, rusts cars, which end up on the scrap heap, which is hauled off by other freighters bound for South Korea, for melting down into Hyundais — which wind up back on our roads. It's a cycle of death and renewal every bit as tidy and self-contained as that played out by the trees we had just seen — only, we decided, not nearly as fetching nor as soothing.

– Leslie Robinson and Alexander Wolff

Editors' Picks for Portsmouth

General Information

Greater Portsmouth Chamber of Commerce, P.O. Box 239, Portsmouth, NH 03801. 603-436-1118. (www.portcity.org)

Where to Stay

Bow Street Inn, 121 Bow St., Portsmouth, NH 03801. 603-431-7760. The only waterfront inn in the city is housed in a historic brewery. Downtown galleries, eateries, and historic sites are a scenic stroll away. Open year-round. Expanded continental breakfast included. $89-$161.

Oracle House Inn, 38 Marcy St., Portsmouth, NH 03801. 603-433-8827. Take a 1702 house, restore each room down to the paint colors, furnish it with period furniture, and set it next to Strawbery Banke, a living-history museum. You'll dream in Colonial vernacular. Open year-round. Breakfast included. $99-$149.

Where to Eat

Dunfey's aboard the *John Wanamaker,* moored under Memorial Bridge, Harbor Place, Portsmouth. 603-433-3111. Sit up on deck or by the gleaming engine, order fancy fish, and be well-heeled for an evening. Open May-Columbus Day daily for lunch and dinner; Columbus Day-April Tuesday-Saturday for dinner only. $$-$$$.

The Stockpot, 53 Bow St., Portsmouth. 603-431-1851. Since 1982, this place has been serving "good food cheap." Soups, sandwiches, entrées, tangy steamed mussels, and the city's best chowder, enjoyed on the outdoor deck or by windows looking out on the Piscataqua River. Open year-round daily 11 A.M.-11:30 P.M. $.

What to See

Prescott Park, off Marcy St., Portsmouth. This seaside green space is perfect for a stroll, a picnic, or a nap. The colorful, ever-blooming All-American Show Garden is where winners are grown for display. There's free music and entertainment throughout the summer.

Strawbery Banke, 64 Marcy St., Portsmouth. 603-433-1100. Buildings, furnishings, and trades from the 1600s to the 1950s make this an enriching stop. Gardens are true to their eras, and a fully provisioned 1943 grocery store has been restored down to the ration cards. Open April-November daily 10-5. $12, children 7-17 $8, under 7 free, families $28. (www.strawberybanke.org)

Portsmouth Harbor Cruises, Ceres Street Dock, 64 Ceres St., Portsmouth. 800-776-0915, 603-436-8084. The 49-passenger *Heritage* offers narrated cruises May-October daily. Harbor cruises $12, children under 18 $8, 2 and under free. Isles of Shoals cruises $16, children $9, 2 and under free.

$\mathcal{O}$ur Grandest Hotels

Sleeping in White Mountain Magnificence

"*A RECIPE FOR AS PERFECT MENTAL AND CORPOREAL* repose as is attainable in this mortal life," reads a quote from an 1869 letter describing a stay in the White Mountains. At the time, northern New Hampshire was the most popular vacation destination for 19th-century Americans. Believing the high mountain air to be healthy, visitors flocked, and savvy hoteliers realized there was gold in them hills. Tourist gold.

By 1880 the hoteliers had transformed their modest inns into the grand resorts of the White Mountains. Numbering at least 19, most with more than 350 rooms, these wooden palaces offered sublime mountain settings and views. Guest rooms were modest, but space was lavish in elegant public areas in which to see and, more important, be seen. Gingerbread flourishes often hid fast and cheap construction; small wonder these establishments had a habit of self-combusting.

But until the flames and the motor car spelled their demise, the grand resorts delivered on the promise of "perfect mental and corporeal repose." Guests arrived by train and stayed for the season to hike, ride horseback, play the newfangled game of golf, and dress to the nines for dinner. That style of travel is gone, and many of the resorts are, too. But a handful remain to offer the mountain air and the glory of yesteryear. Their long hallways are home to the ghosts of dowagers and debutantes, of guests such as Winston Churchill and Mark Twain. Today you can play golf or tennis, get a massage or rent a mountain bike, take a swim or retreat to a veranda rocking chair. No ordinary hotels, these resorts offer all the amenities — along with a history lesson in Americans' love of leisure.

The Balsams

Set on 15,000 acres, the Balsams' immense building can accommodate 425 guests a gazillion miles from anywhere. It's at least four hours from Boston, around 12 miles from Canada, and light-years away from just about everything else. Tucked into the isolated northern tip of New Hampshire, it has been able to carry on the grand traditions of the past in grand style.

Like any self-respecting New England building, the Balsams is an amalgam. Nestled in the granite thrusts of Dixville Notch, it began in 1866 as the Dix House with 25 rooms. By 1896 a barn had been converted; in 1910 the clapboard west wing was added; eight years later the concrete Hampshire House expanded the room count to today's 221.

For all its size, the Balsams feels intimate, its warren of hallways and tangle of rooms presenting a pleasant navigational challenge. In one of those rooms, the citizens of

Dixville Notch are the first in the country to cast their ballots in presidential elections. The ballroom is now converted to an attractive nightclub-style room. On the ground level is the resort's own movie theater, which does double duty as a sanctified chapel. Throughout the hotel are pictures, maps, letters, and other memorabilia relating to its long past. Guest rooms — varying greatly from small to almost large — are prettily decorated with either bright wallpaper or fresh paint, wicker chairs, and painted wood dressers.

Outside, lawns slope to the pool and man-made (1900) Lake Gloriette, stocked with canoes and paddleboats. Three tennis courts are clay; three, all-weather plexicushion. Recent additions to the resort's leisure offerings include an exercise room and a beauty shop with a massage therapist on staff. Even nongolfers must drive up to the Panorama Club-

Family relay races, golf, hiking, and swimming are among the summer activities offered at the Balsams Grand Resort Hotel. (*courtesy the Balsams*)

house, base for the 18-hole, par 72 Donald Ross course designed in 1912. Aptly named, the clubhouse affords a view that reaches to Vermont and Canada. The course, golfers, has a slope rating ranging from 124 to 136.

But you can enjoy the outdoors without chasing a ball by joining one of the hikes or walking tours given by the resident naturalist. Or you can park yourself in a rocking chair on the red-roofed veranda and park the kids in the daylong supervised program that's offered during the "Social Season" of July Fourth weekend through Labor Day.

Service in the old style put the Balsams on the map, and what keeps it there is its dining room. The setting — lace curtains; Corinthian columns topped with gold; the evening's entire menu of appetizers, entrées, salads, and desserts displayed on a tiered table at room's center — is as impressive as the cooking. The old resorts prided themselves on the quality of their cuisine, and dining at the Balsams remains first-rate. One is grateful, though, that meals, while bountiful, are not on the scale of those served in resorts in the late 1800s: seven courses. Three times a day.

The Mount Washington

Unlike the Balsams, which shoulders up to the mountains, the Mount Washington Hotel, opened in 1902, rises from a valley floor. With its white walls, dark red roofs, and flying pennants, it looks like a fairy princess's castle.

This is impressive: Nine hundred feet of wide veranda encircle the hotel, the eastern stretch a front-row view of 6,288-foot Mount Washington. The main lobby has 23-foot ceilings and nine pairs of soaring columns. Beyond is the conservatory, facing east. To the south is the ballroom, to the north the octagonal dining room that assures virtually everyone a view and a "good" table.

Throughout is the handiwork of the 250 Italian craftsmen who created plaster garlands, braids, and rosettes. On the ground level is an indoor swimming pool, as well as the former speakeasy. (Many of these resorts thrived during Prohibition with bootleg gin smuggled in from Canada.)

History oozes: The Bretton Woods Conference, which established the world gold standard, was held here approximately 50 years ago. On many guest-room doors bronze plaques name illustrious former occupants, such as John Maynard Keynes and Rod Laver. Woodrow Wilson and Joseph Kennedy also graced the resort with their presence.

Between the veranda and New England's highest peak are the outdoor pool, a concert stage, 12 clay tennis courts, walking and hiking paths, and some of the Mount Washington's 27 holes of golf. Also on the property is a Victorian stable, a stone chapel, and the resort's own printing press. A supervised program keeps youngsters 5 to 12 occupied daily. The dining room, painted its original flattering shade of pink, features the Fred Petra band during dinner.

Every summer, in a tradition that began nine years ago, the Mount Washington turns back the clock with a Great Gatsby Weekend. Guests dress up in vintage clothing to stroll the conservatory, the great lobby, and the ballroom. They return, for an evening, to the days when ladies seemed to float along the ground and happiness was a waltz with a pomaded partner under the Tiffany windows of a grand resort ballroom.

– Janice Brand

Editors' Picks for the White Mountains

General Information

Mount Washington Valley Chamber of Commerce, Main St., P.O. Box 2300, North Conway, NH 03860. 800-367-3364, 603-356-3171. (www.4seasonresort.com)

Northern White Mountain Chamber of Commerce, 164 Main St., P.O. Box 298, Berlin, NH 03570. 800-992-7480, 603-752-6060. (www.northernwhitemountains.com)

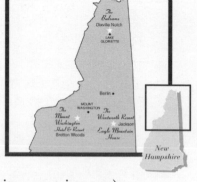

Where to Stay

The Balsams Grand Resort Hotel, Dixville Notch, NH 03576. 800-255-0600 (outside N.H.), 800-255-0800. Open late May to mid-October and late December to late March. As on a cruise ship, all meals, activities, entertainment, lecture series — everything except liquor — are included. $185-$215. (www.thebalsams.com)

The Mount Washington Hotel & Resort, Rte. 302, Bretton Woods, NH 03575. 800-258-0330, 603-278-1000. The country inn, motor inn, and town homes are open year-round; the hotel is open late May to late October. Full breakfast and dinner included. A number of packages are available. $210-$1,195. (www.mtwashington.com)

Two other hotels with roots in the grand resort tradition are:

Eagle Mountain House, Carter Notch Rd., Jackson, NH 03846. 800-966-5779, 603-383-9111. The Eagle Mountain House dates from 1879, but the original structure burned in 1915. The present building dates to 1916 and 1929. There are 93 rooms (decorated with four-poster beds, down coverlets, and armoires), nine-hole golf, tennis, a pool, and an exercise room. The feel inside is very updated, but the building, the veranda with big rockers, and the view of Wildcat Valley remain much the same as in the golden days. Open year-round. Packages with meals included are available. Without meals: $59-$159. (www.eaglemt.com)

The Wentworth Resort, P.O. Box M, Jackson, NH 03846. 800-637-0013, 603-383-9700. In the 1880s Wentworth Hall commanded Jackson with its grand porte cochere, casino, and numerous shingle-style buildings. Today the main building, its veranda hung with geraniums, has 28 modestly decorated rooms. The Arden House, built in 1880 with wide French doors and a lush suite, has 15 more rooms. The resort's room count totals 58. The adjacent golf course is not owned by the resort, and condominiums behind the hotel were built in an effort to stave off bankruptcy that occurred in 1971. Today Fritz Koeppel is restoring and updating. Open year-round. Breakfast and a full, five-course dinner (in the resort's four-diamond restaurant) are included in the rates. $149-$259. (www.sih.ch/actimemb/wentnh.htm)

Angling for Moose

Northern New Hampshire Is
Where the Wild Things Are

HOT JULY SUN IS IN MY EYES AS I WIND MY WAY PAST Lancaster on Route 3, penetrating northernmost New Hampshire. I haven't been here for some time — 20 years, perhaps. Back then, I was riding high above the road in the passenger seat of my brother Johnny's box truck. That is the vantage point from which I saw my first moose.

These uppermost reaches of the state are different in character than all of the land to the south; not for lack of development, though that is surely the case, but because this is where New Hampshire jetties into the vast pine timberlands spanning northern New York, half of Maine, and much of adjoining Canada. The Great North Woods.

Route 3 eventually crosses the Canadian border. Most

Author Carol Connare has seen many moose in northern New Hampshire. She photographed this cow and her babies from the Connecticut River. *(photo by Carol Connare)*

of the way it is flanked by swamps and woods and wetlands — perfect moose environs. In May, when the blackflies get feisty and push the animals out toward the road, drivers learn why Route 3 is called Moose Alley.

It was an early May morning, and Johnny and I had come to deliver tires (our family's business). Fueled by coffee and doughnuts, we'd been on the road for over three hours, heading away from our home in southern New Hampshire. We were listening to Casey Kasem's Top 40 when out of the corner of my eye, I saw him. The moose was galloping in the grass by the road, right alongside us. His stride matched ours for about 15 seconds, and I got a good, long look at him. Luckily, he veered off into the woods instead of into our path. "Did you see that?!" I said, my eyes as big as saucers. My brother laughed at his little sister's awe.

Johnny is gone now; he died of a brain tumor at age 25. And since that first moose I have seen many, many more, mostly when I lived in Alaska. Now I head to Pittsburg to probe the headwater region of the Connecticut River, to re-connect with family memories, and to find moose.

The houses thin out the farther north I go, farms sprawl, skidders sit idle. I remember how Johnny would come to Pittsburg to deliver tires, but he also came to Pittsburg for pleasure. Every summer he would spend a week here, plying the waters of Lake Francis for salmon and trout. He was, by design, a bass fisherman, but the cold streams and lakes of Pittsburg called his name nevertheless. I didn't get to go on those trips. I was just a pesky sister. But I would eagerly await his return to hear fish stories, see his tanned, relaxed smile, and find out what treasure he'd brought me: a loon T-shirt, a moose key chain, or a pretty rock from one of the lakes. Lake Francis was the only place in the world he liked to fish better than Lake Contoocook in Rindge, New Hampshire, where our family cottage is located. It was the only time he ever truly left his work behind.

Johnny was a mechanic. The kind who didn't charge for the little stuff — the kind who fixed nuns' cars for free. He always kept his tackle box and rod ready to go in the trunk of his Impala. "Why don't you buy American?" he would scold me for my appetite for German cars. "They're a lot cheaper to maintain," he'd say with the authority of a father. Though I am not much of a fisherman, for this trip I have placed his tackle box and pole in the trunk of my Volkswagen.

First, I get lost in Colebrook, too busy checking out storefronts to stay on Route 3. Seems like there's no shortage of state liquor stores up here. My thoughts turn to Mike Berry, a logger I once worked with down in Woodstock for a winter. He had grown up in Colebrook and learned how to log in these woods. He lives in Thornton now, and I think about how, to him, nearby Lincoln must feel like a big city compared with his hometown.

Mike and I have argued about logging in the North Woods. I believe there is a need for protective measures, for some alternatives to clearcutting. Incentives are needed to encourage the replanting of heavily forested lands. But how do you ask whole communities and generations of families to rethink their way of life? It's a rare kind of fore-sight that's needed to keep these woods viable for future generations. I think these thoughts as I drive by the Wasau Paper Company Mill.

The 300 square miles of land known as Pittsburg, a township larger in acreage than the entire state of Rhode Island, once was a nation unto itself, with its own currency and government. The Indian Stream Territory was established in 1832 during the border dispute between Canada and the United States and dissolved a short decade later. Now most of the land is owned by the Champion Paper Company. According to Buster Hutchins, proprietor of Wilderness Sporting Goods of Pittsburg, there were a 100 skidders working these woods until five years ago.

"Now there's about eight. It's been cleaned off pretty good," Hutchins tells me (as I now poke around his store); he himself worked in the woods for 35 years before opening his store in the late 1980s. "A few years ago, operations were cut back. You can barely walk in the woods around here because of the heavy scrub growth. It's a crying shame."

Now tourism is the economy's main source of fuel in Pittsburg, home to roughly 600 people. On a good summer weekend, about 2,000 visitors arrive looking for the kind of remote peace, quiet, and recreation only a place like Pitts-burg can offer. The daunting acreage of Lake Francis, Back Lake, and the three Connecticut Lakes, plus the clean, heady aroma given off by the pine forest, are a powerful elixir for world-weary visitors. Except for tidy housekeeping cabins, a few lodges, and a handful of houses, the lakes are pristine. For now, at least.

Salmon and trout lure fisherman to the region, but

there are many other pleasures in Pittsburg: biking, hiking, moose-spotting on the road to Canada, swimming, sailing. The first item on my agenda is to do absolutely nothing at all. Maybe I'll pick wild raspberries, listen for a loon, settle on the porch of my cabin for an afternoon of reading or day-dreaming. When I'm no longer wild around the eyes, I will take a dip in Garfield Falls and hike to the top of Magalloway Mountain for views into Maine, Canada, and Vermont. I also plan to visit the Fourth Connecticut Lake, the very begin-ning of the Connecticut River.

But for now, I need to address Lake Francis. It's the most southerly body of water in Pittsburg and is named for Saint Francis, the patron saint of wildlife. Indeed, beaver, hawks, eagles, osprey, heron, otter, fisher cat, and of course, moose call this country home.

Moose are herbivores that stand in the water for hours eating sodium-rich vegetation. An adult can eat 40 to 60 pounds of plants a day. (photo by Carol Connare)

"It's overpopulated with moose up here," Hutchins says. On this particular day he has just finished dressing off 700 pounds of roadkill. At the Moose Festival, held annually in late August, mock moose stew is on the menu, but locals eat the real thing because animals often get whacked by motorists. I vow to come back for the three-day festival celebrating the resident ruminant, with a moose-calling contest, an auto show, a Mardi Gras parade, dances, moose cruises, a street fair, and a multitude of moose memorabilia.

I continue to work my way around Hutchins's shop now and find a little bit of everything. He offers flies tied by six different local people, live bait, and a wide array of camping and boating supplies, and he also rents canoes. There's always free coffee and doughnuts in his shop and an inspiring collection of photos chronicling hunting and fishing successes.

Hutchins and another fellow put out a map and guide of fly-fishing waters in and around Pittsburg that names all the pools along the river. Some parts are catch and release only, from others you can take home salmon and trout to grill up for dinner.

Here in the friendliest town south of the border (never mind its being the *only* town south of the border), the fish may elude you, but the peace and quiet won't. I don't know how long I'd been sitting at the dam on the lake, looking out across the wide, wild water. For at least an hour I guess. The clear blue of it reminds me of Lake Louise in Banff, where the water is the color of tourmalines. Again my thoughts turn to Johnny. Now I understand why he escaped up here. And I reconsider something Hutchins said to me that I had passed off as a cliché. "You don't have to go to church to get to heaven," he told me. "It's right here."

I whisper out across the water. "Hey Johnny, you'd better save some of the fish for the rest of us."

– Carol Connare

Editors' Picks for
Pittsburgh and Vicinity

General Information

North Country Chamber of Commerce, Box 1, Colebrook, NH 03576. 603-237-8939.

Connecticut Lakes Tourist Association, P.O. Box 38, Pittsburg, NH 03592. 603-538-7405.

The Pittsburg Trading Post, Rte. 3, P.O. Box 187, Pittsburg, NH 03592. 603-538-6533.

Wilderness Sporting Goods, Beach Rd., P.O. Box 222, Pittsburg, NH 03592. 603-538-7166.

Where to Stay and Eat

Tall Timber Lodge, off Rte. 3 on Back Lake, 231 Beach Rd., Pittsburg, NH 03592. 800-835-6343, 603-538-6651. Founded in 1946 by North Country guide Vernon Hawes, the Caron family carries on the same rustic, relaxing tradition. There are eight rooms in the lodge — two with private baths; 17 cabins and cottages, some with luxury amenities including cathedral ceilings, wood-burning fireplaces, barbecue grills, fully equipped kitchens, VCRs, stereos with CD players, and Jacuzzis. Private porches and decks provide scenic views of Back Lake and the surrounding hills. Meals are served in the sporting-camp tradition — one selection at each meal — but children and vegetarians are accommodated. There's also a resident fly-fishing guide. Open year-round. Breakfast and dinner included. $32-$220, average price per person per weekend night $65. Special packages available. (www.talltimbcr.com)

The Glen, 77 The Glen Rd. (nine miles north of Pittsburg village), Pittsburg, NH 03592. 800-445-4536, 603-538-6500. A full-service sporting lodge for half a century. Choose spacious rooms with private bath, or rustic log cottages, with three country-cooked meals daily served in a fireplaced dining room. Open May 15 to October 15. All three meals included. $70-$86.50.

Lake Francis State Campground, River Rd. (off Rte. 3), 7 miles north of Pittsburg village, Pittsburg, NH 03592. 603-538-6965. There are 42 campsites located beside the 2,000-acre man-made lake, including five walk-in sites. Most can accommodate self-contained RVs. The campground is equipped with a boat launch and picnic area. Open mid-May to Columbus Day. $12-$16.

Massachusetts

Nobska Lighthouse, Woods Hole. (photo by J. Latching, courtesy Falmouth Chamber of Commerce)

It's the Best Day of the Year

Patriots Day in Boston

PATRIOTS DAY IS A HOLIDAY PECULIAR TO NEW ENGLAND — a day my brother, who was born on Patriots Day, once believed was the Massachusetts way of saying "Happy birthday, Tom." From the beginning, my parents sort of encouraged the confusion. They named him Thomas Paul. Thomas for Jefferson. Paul for Revere.

My family isn't the only one to hold Patriots Day — once April 19, now officially the first Monday after Easter — in high esteem. It is perhaps the quintessential New England day, a celebration of spring, revolution, human athletic endeavor, and time off. It is a day, more than anything, in which one attempts to do as much as possible in the daylight hours.

I had a plan. I'd begin before sunup, to witness the annual reenactment of the Battle of Lexington and Concord and the start of the Revolutionary War. I'd ride with Paul Revere out of the North End (I on bike and he on horse), catch the Red Sox at Fenway, and see the runners off in Hopkinton, the starting line for the Boston Marathon. I'd do other stuff, too. I'd pack light.

Lexington Green, 5:30 A.M. It is dark, but I am not alone. I park my car at the Stop & Shop a quarter mile away and fall in with a sleepy pilgrimage of families, roller skaters, and bicyclists headed up Bedford Street to the green. The bell from the Old Belfry is ringing the alarm, and most of Lexington seems to have heeded it.

In anticipation of the British arrival — it's nearing six now and a misty dawn light is rising — parents and grandparents test-hoist the little ones about halfway up to shoulders. In a minute or two things will be asked of those shoulders, lower backs, and biceps that are asked only once a year. There is a sea of people now, thousands, and just in case the partisan crowd — a man parades with a sign "Limeys Go Home" — is a bit rusty on the events of April 19, 1775, Captain John Parker provides a synopsis. A *shhh* spreads over the great green, and those without a ladder or long legs sprint for higher ground. The British are coming.

Actually, the revolutionary scout appears first, alerting the regulars at Buckman Tavern. The redcoats line up in crisp formation on the green. The minutemen look as if they'd just as soon backpedal to Concord.

"Hold your ground, boys!" urges an older lady to my left. The British order the rebels to disperse. The minutemen don't, and somebody — mind you, I was watching closely — fires the first shot. Dozens of muskets crackle, the acrid smell of gunpowder rises, and a cloud of smoke billows out. The War of Independence is on, and I'm off.

Hopkinton, 7:45 A.M. The first bus of Boston Marathon runners arrives at Hopkinton High School at about 8:00 A.M., and I'm there to meet it. Cops are drinking coffee in huge clutches, and if Dave McGillivray isn't, he should be. He is the technical coordinator of the marathon, which is no mean feat around noon when you've got TV helicopters buzzing in and out, zillions of runners stuffed onto Main Street (the folks in the back will take ten minutes just to cross the starting line), and spectators piling out of pancake breakfasts, predawn house parties, and flea markets.

Actually, McGillivray's official duties don't end until the conclusion of the marathon. At that moment, McGillivray returns to Hopkinton and toes the starting line at about 6:00 P.M., the last official starter to Boston's most famous race. He finishes around 10:00, has a nightcap, and presumably wakes up sometime in midsummer. Last year was his 26th straight year at this.

Me, I make a quick review of the Hopkinton proceedings. I note a child with cotton candy. And though I'm running late, I decide to sample the pancake breakfast fare prepared by the Lions Club. Things are just getting rolling when I hear the static of a police radio and an announcement

Redcoats cross the North Bridge during a reenactment of the Battle of Lexington. *(photo by Dennis Dostie, courtesy Greater Merrimack Valley Convention and Visitors Bureau)*

that the roads to and from Hopkinton are now officially closed. Uh-oh.

"Where do you think you're going?" asks a cop who has waved me over from an attempted left-hand turn onto Main Street toward the Mass. Pike. I tell him I need to get out of town: I'm bound for the North End and Paul Revere. "The ride to Lexington?" he asks.

"That's the one," I say.

The officer lets me go. He knows all about Patriots Day.

Heartbreak Hill, 10:00 A.M. I'd originally thought about riding my bike the entire marathon route, but time won't stand for that. Instead, I park my car in Newton, take my bike out of the trunk, and ride over the famed Heartbreak Hill, where spectators have already set down lawn chairs, portable radios, coolers, and magazine stacks. It is here, at the race's 20-mile mark, where the Boston Marathon is traditionally won or lost.

I take it to be cosmic intervention that as I pedal furiously down Causeway Street and past old Boston Garden, I hear a police siren, a strange click-clack of hoofs on asphalt, and there he is: Paul Revere, tricornered hat, knickers, and ponytail, passing under the expressway en route for the suburbs.

"The British are coming, the British are coming!" he shouts gamely. No, what is coming is an MBTA bus, which presents obvious difficulties both for Paul, who's attempting to cross the very narrow, construction-choked Charlestown bridge, and a foolhardy bicyclist trying to ask him questions. In between the calls to arms, Paul Revere notes with just a touch of fatigue that the ride out of Boston surely hasn't gotten any easier in 200 plus years.

Fenway Park, noon. Paul Revere may have his troubles, but nothing like long-suffering Red Sox fans who've waited the better part of a century for a World Series victory. It's the second inning when I get to Fenway, the marathon has started, and Boston is playing pennant favorite Toronto. It is the usual festive Patriots Day crowd, with half the fans nuzzled up against transistor radios for marathon updates; the

Patriots prepare for battle at a minutemen reenactment. *(photo by Dennis Dostie, courtesy Greater Merrimack Valley Convention and Visitors Bureau)*

other half are dads telling sons, some of whom are weeks old, the particulars of the infield-fly rule.

The Sox tie the game 4-4 in the eighth — about the same time the lead runners are coming up Beacon Street for the homestretch. They'll be in Kenmore Square, right outside the ballpark and a mile from the finish, in ten minutes. Stay or go? Thousands of us weigh the chances of the Sox coming through. Spring optimism reigns. Most of the crowd stays. I stay. The Sox lose on a balk and a rock.

Kenmore Square, 3:30 P.M. By the time I get to the square, the runners are passing by in waves. The top finishers were here an hour and a half ago. I am not dismayed. VCRs, programmed by talented friends, were made for moments like this.

Patriots Day is coming to a close. I have missed a few things: the swan boats in Boston Common, a walk along the Freedom Trail. But when the sun sets, I'm exactly where I want to be. I'm on my bike again, riding along the Charles River as scullers, sailors, in-line skaters, runners, picnickers, walkers, and inveterate Big Dayers show no signs of quitting. Daylight is precious. It's the best day of the year.

– Todd Balf

Editors' Picks for
Greater Boston

General Information

Greater Boston Convention and Visitors Bureau, 2 Copley Pl., Suite 105, Boston, MA 02116. 800-888-5515, 617-536-4100. (www.bostonusa.com)

Concord Chamber of Commerce, 2 Lexington Rd., Concord, MA 01742. 978-369-3120.

Lexington Visitor's Center, 1875 Massachusetts Ave., Lexington, MA 02173. 781-862-1450. Open May-October daily 9-5, November-April daily 10-3.

Boston Athletic Association, 131 Clarendon St., 8th Floor, Boston, MA, 02116. 617-236-1652. (www.bostonmarathon.org)

Where to Stay

Concord's Colonial Inn, 48 Monument Sq., Concord, MA 01742. 800-370-9200, 978-369-9200. This 1716 Colonial-style house overlooks Concord green, where the famous battle took place. Some of the 49 rooms have exposed-beam ceilings and hardwood floors. Open year-round. $125-$185. Breakfast, lunch, and dinner served in the dining room. $$-$$$. (www.concordscolonialinn.com)

Hawthorne Inn, 462 Lexington Rd., Concord, MA 01742.

978-369-5610. Situated along famed Battle Road of 1775, this 1870 Italianate Colonial is on land once belonging to Ralph Emerson, the Alcotts, and Nathaniel Hawthorne. The latter contributed two trees, currently on property, from England. Seven rooms with private baths are decorated with antique and modern art. Open year-round. Continental breakfast included. $150-$215.

Timothy Jones House, 231 Concord Rd., Bedford, MA 01730. 781-275-8579. Lieutenant Timothy Jones, a Revolutionary soldier, built this Georgian country home in 1775. There are three rooms, two suites, and eight working fireplaces as well as wide-pine floors, hand-hewn beams and hardware, antiques, and quilts. Guests can walk to Concord Bridge through the Great Meadows Wildlife Refuge. Open year-round. Continental breakfast and afternoon tea included. $85-$120.

Where to Eat

Durgin-Park, 30 North Market St., Faneuil Hall Marketplace, Boston. 617-227-2038. Durgin-Park's communal tables and Yankee menu have changed little since the days when its customers were mostly fishermen and longshoremen. Open daily for lunch and dinner; no reservations. $$.

Union Oyster House, 41 Union St., Boston. 978-227-2750. America's oldest restaurant (1826) is housed in a building dating back to pre-Revolutionary days. It is located on the Freedom Trail and features New England-style seafood and broiled meats. Daniel Webster was a regular, and JFK had his own booth. Open Sunday-Thursday 11-9:30; Friday-Saturday 11-10. Union Bar open until midnight. $$-$$$.

What to See

Paul Revere House, 19 North Sq., Boston. 617-523-2338. On the night of April 18, 1775, silversmith Paul Revere left his small wooden home in Boston's North End and set out on a journey that would make him into a legend. It is downtown Boston's oldest building. Open mid-April to October 31, daily 9:30-5:15; November-April 14, 9:30-4:15; closed Mondays January-March and holidays. $2.50, seniors and students $2, children 5-17 $1. (www.paulreverehouse.org)

Buckman Tavern, 1 Bedford Rd., Lexington. 781-862-5598. See where the minutemen first mustered at midnight and waited for the Regulars to arrive. On display are 18th-century muskets, cookware, and furniture, as well as a bullet hole through a door. Open April-October Monday-Saturday 10-5, Sunday 1-5 P.M. $4, children 6-16 $2.

Fenway Park, Yawkey Way, Boston. 617-236-6666 for tours, 617-267-8661 for ticket office. Real baseball on real grass, complete with the Green Monster. Season begins early April, ends in late September. Guided one-hour tours Monday-Friday 10-2 (last tour at 1 P.M.). $5, seniors $4, children 15 and under $3.

Freedom Trail, Boston National Historical Park Visitor Center, 15 State St., Boston. 617-242-5642. Wear comfortable shoes and pick up a map here, then follow the red stripe connecting Boston's most historic sites (including the Paul Revere House and the Old North Church, where those two famous lanterns were hung) along a three-mile path. Open daily 9-6, free walking tours and some guided tours.

Minute Man National Historical Park, 174 Liberty St., Concord. 978-369-6944. Two sites recall the opening shots of the Revolution: Battle Road preserves part of the path of fleeing British troops; the North Bridge marks where Emerson's "embattled farmers" stood. Minute Man Visitor Center, Lexington; open daily 9-5; free. North Bridge Visitor Center, 508-369-6993; open daily 9-5:30; free.

Birding by Bike on Plum Island

A Day at the Parker River Wildlife Refuge

AS I APPROACH THE PARKER RIVER BRIDGE, A MALE marsh hawk slowly quarters the salt marsh, a gently rocking, seemingly lazy flight but as precise and purposeful as that of a falcon. The hawk flushes a cluster of sandpipers, which reassemble in a tightly packed, wedged-shaped flock that vanishes behind the bank of a distant tidal creek. I shift gears on my mountain bike and glide onto Plum Island, leaving the Massachusetts mainland behind me.

My destination this May morning is the luxuriant southern half of the island, the Parker River National Wildlife Refuge, an avian bed-and-breakfast for more than

250 species of migratory birds. The refuge's 4,700 acres include salt marsh, sand dunes, and freshwater wetlands. There are also six miles of glorious beach, footpaths, boardwalks, and a couple of observation towers. A level seven-mile road, part paved, part dirt, caters to slow-moving cars — which makes biking safe — and passes through some of the best birding sites in New England.

I lock my bike in the first lot and follow the boardwalk to the ocean. A wave buckles and sends a cold spray far up the beach. A congregation of sanderlings scurries, but gulls, as patient as ever, heed the ill-tempered sea — three species, three age classes, nine plumages — like a crowd at a potluck. A loon drifts by, face in the water, hunting. A few eiders bob in the whitecaps, lobster buoys dressed in down. A line of white-winged scoters passes just above the distant swells.

Later, pedaling south, I stop at the salt pans, a series of brackish pools surrounded by crisp brown cord grass along the west side of the road. The tide is high. Phlegmatic

black-bellied and semipalmated plovers, both in bright breeding plumage, crowd a small, grassy isle, while longer-legged, more animated greater yellowlegs waltz through the shallows striking at fish. A bevy of short-billed dowitchers probe the mud for worms, as a flock of dunlins arrows in. Black ducks and green-winged teals idle along the far shore. A great blue heron rises like a periscope from the marsh, and a flock of birders, cars in a line, celebrate.

A mute swan, one of many birds regularly seen on Plum Island. (photo by *Kindra Clineff*)

Like shallow water in the salt pans, time drains away, so I continue on past dunes robed in beach plum and bayberry, past a stand of pitch pines. I stop and click off a half-dozen songbirds — rufous-sided towhee, yellow-rumped warbler, robin, catbird, blue jay, white-throated sparrow — collectively a manifestation of the season, a calendar with wings.

Reaching Hellcat Swamp at lunchtime, three miles to go, I have these options to consider: an observation tower overlooking the freshwater impoundment; a marsh trail; a boardwalk through a tupelo swamp — where I once saw a red fox with a rabbit in its mouth — or a loop trail across the road, over dunes, through a swale and a winterberry swamp to a scenic ocean view. Three crows call loudly from above the pines. I listen and follow, lunch forgotten.

– Ted Levin

Editors' Picks for Plum Island and Newburyport

General Information

Greater Newburyport Chamber of Commerce, 29 State St., Newburyport, MA 01950. 978-462-6680. (www.newburyport.chamber.org)

Parker River National Wildlife Refuge, off Rte. 1A, Plum Island, Newbury, MA 01950. 978-465-5753. Open year-round, sunrise to sunset. $5 per car or free with a federal duck stamp; $2 to walk or bike in. Annual and seasonal passes available.

Where to Stay

Walton's Ocean Front, 20 Fordham Way, Newbury, MA 01950. 978-465-7171. Walton's is the only lodging on Plum Island. Located just six buildings down from the wildlife refuge, it offers 17 units in cottages and apartments on the beach. Historic downtown Newburyport is three miles away. Open year-round. $50-$280. (www.newburyport.net)

Clark Currier Inn, 45 Green St., Newburyport, MA 01950. 978-465-8363. This charming eight-room bed-and-breakfast conveys the grace of a bygone era. All rooms have private baths and are furnished with fine antiques. Open year-round. Continental breakfast included. $95-$145.

The Garrison Inn, 11 Brown Sq., Newburyport, MA 01950. 978-499-8500. Constructed in 1809, the Garrison Inn is now on the National Register as a Historic Landmark. The 24 guest rooms and suites are appointed with reproductions and antiques, yet offer modern conveniences such as private baths, telephones, and televisions. Open year-round. Continental breakfast included. $98-$175. The dining room (see David's below) is open nightly for dinner. (www.garrison-inn.com)

The Windsor House, 38 Federal St., Newburyport, MA 01950. 888-873-5296, 978-462-3778. Each room tells a story from the 1786 brick beauty's earliest days. Taste a bit of Old England during tea and breakfast. There are four large guest rooms, all with private baths. Open year-round. Full two-course cooked English breakfast included. $135. (www.virtualcities.com)

Where to Eat

David's, 11 Brown Sq., Newburyport. 978-462-8077. Parents, treat yourself to a food-fight-free meal and a gourmet dinner. David's will watch your children while they eat kid foods in a separate dining room downstairs stuffed with toys and movies. You get to choose from two other dining rooms, one downstairs with an American menu; $-$$. Or a more formal spot upstairs, serving a continental menu; $$-$$$. Downstairs is open Monday-Friday for lunch; daily for dinner. Upstairs is open daily for dinner. Child care $5 per child for ages 18 months and older.

Glenn's Restaurant & Cool Bar, 44 Merrimac St., Newburyport. 978-465-3811. Changing daily menus in a California bistro style. Choose from Oriental, Southwestern, and Caribbean cuisine, among others. Watch as your dish is prepared in the open kitchen to the tune of live blues piano on Thursday and Sunday nights. Blues jams with special guests Sunday evenings 7-10 P.M. Open daily for dinner. $$$-$$$$.

Scandia Restaurant, 25 State St., Newburyport. 978-462-6271. This cozy Victorian-style restaurant furnished with antiques, gold-trimmed mirrors, and dark hardwood floors is known widely for its Sunday brunch (mid-October to Mother's Day) featuring eggs Florentine, Belgian waffles, and homemade breads. Lunch and dinner are just as delicious. Open Monday-Friday for lunch and dinner, Saturday and Sunday for breakfast and dinner. $$-$$$.

What to See

Massachusetts Audubon Society, 10 State St., Newburyport. 978-462-9998. These are only the temporary digs for what will be the society's largest interpretive facility yet. Joppa Flats Education Center and Wildlife Sanctuary is being built on the Plum Island Turnpike and is scheduled to open in the year 2000. Currently the society offers a variety of adult- and family-oriented natural-history programs. Call for schedule of events and fees.

Air Plum Island, Plum Island Turnpike, Newbury. 978-462-2114. If you've come to see birds, why not see things their way? Aerial tours offered afternoons and weekends, plus introductory lessons in ultralights. Lighthouse tours (30 minutes, six to seven lighthouses) $75 for up to three people; hour-long tour $130; 15-minute tours available.

The Birdwatcher of Newburyport, 50 Water St., Newburyport. 978-462-2473. Located in the Tannery shopping mall in downtown Newburyport, this shop caters to birders and sponsors guided walks. Open year-round Monday-Wednesday 9:30-6, Thursday until 8 P.M., Friday-Saturday until 6:30 P.M.

The Beaches of Chatham

A Beach for Every Day on Cape Cod's Eastern Tip

THE SEA HAS ALWAYS HAD THIS POWER: TO CHANGE the ordinary into beauty. For us, too, the sea and its tumbled sand rubs smooth our troubles, and washed ashore, we feel, for awhile at least, as lovely as driftwood or sea glass or shining shards of fish bone.

It is why, of course, we still seek the summer Cape, despite the snarled traffic on U.S. Route 6 — the "Mid-Cape Highway" — that on weekends sometimes holds us nearly still until we finally reach the tantalizing shores. Of all the 15 Cape Cod towns, there may be no shores more gratifying than those of Chatham. And perhaps no other place on the

Best Pie Around

Once you've visited Marion's, eating pie will never be the same. This small shop has served Cape Cod guests since 1951. Making old-fashioned two-crust pies, breads, and rolls from scratch is what keeps locals and tourists coming back for more — and more.

Marion's Pie Shop, 2202 Main St., West Chatham. 508-432-9439. Open April-December 24; June-August Tuesday-Saturday 7-6, Sunday 7-2; other months 7-2.

Cape where the sea displays its power for change. Tourists stand today by the Chatham Fish Pier, looking out to the great rift in the barrier beach caused by a January storm in 1987, a scene of unforgettable, disturbing beauty.

The town sits on the eastern tip of the Cape, facing Nantucket Sound to the south, the Atlantic to the east. Its fame comes, in part, from its favored location off the well-beaten Cape Cod trail: "First stop of the east wind," locals say. It is that wind, coupled with rip currents and shoals, that over the centuries has claimed so many ships.

There was a time, two decades past, when you could stroll the Chatham beaches at low tide and discover the stark bones of shipwrecks poking from the sand — wrecks once so numerous that a legendary local beachcomber named "Good Walter" Eldredge built a beach house from the timbers of 17 ships that foundered here.

Chatham has the most coastline of any Cape town, and despite the tourism and inevitable development, despite the town's reputation as one of the Cape's most sophisticated and elegant resorts, it is still a fisherman's home. Over 65 commercial fishing boats dock at Chatham's municipal pier, and you can lie in the deep hot sand and hear the comforting throb of their motors.

***Chatham's Pleasant Street beach has wide, sandy
stretches, perfect for a day of kite-flying.*** *(photo by Bob
Bermudes, courtesy Bermudescenic)*

In summer the wind prevails from the southwest, stir-
ring the surf at Cockle Cove and Harding's Beach and
Ridgevale Beach. A family can choose a different kind of
beach each day of the week: a tidal pond, a beach with
breakers and pounding surf, a beach beside a lighthouse, liv-
ing-room-size strips of sand beside a road, a beach that
stretches far beyond view, a beach along the warm sound or
by the chilled Atlantic.

Boston-area photographer Brian Smith, who had vaca-
tioned since childhood near Falmouth, discovered Chatham
four summers ago when construction on his house forced
him and his family to find a seasonal residence. While his
young children search the beach for treasures, scooping min-
nows and shells into buckets, he looks for light and color and
the moments that turn the Cape beaches into a vast, unend-
ing playground. He has shot, he figures, over 4,000 frames
along the beaches of Chatham. "So many nooks and cran-
nies," he says, "it's almost impossible to know where you're
going all the time."

When you drive the roads with a native, you will in-
evitably hear about the price of this town's beauty. In the

1930s Chatham children walked the beaches alone. The summer hotels filled with Bostonians, but there was so much beach and relatively few tourists. The Chatham children raced their sailing skiffs in the harbor and felt as if the sky and everything beneath it belonged to them. Of course, that has changed forever. The beach brought the changes, and everyone recognizes the irony in that. "The only thing that's the same," said one 11th-generation Chatham native, "is the beach."

– Mel Allen

Editors' Picks for Chatham

General Information

Chatham Chamber of Commerce, 533 Main St., Chatham, MA 02633. 800-715-5567, 508-945-5199. Visitors Center at routes 137 and 28 open May-October daily 10-6, Sunday noon-6. (www.virtualcapecod.com/chambers/chatham.html)

Where to Stay

Chatham Bars Inn, Shore Rd., Chatham, MA 02633. 800-527-4884, 508-945-0096. Built in 1914 as a hunting lodge, this grand oceanfront resort is the picture of elegance. The main inn and cottages are sprinkled over 20 acres and include more than 173 rooms, many with ocean views. Guests can enjoy a private beach, tennis and croquet courts, a nine-hole golf course, a pool, fine dining, and fitness facilities all on site. Open year-round. $190-$1,100. Dining room open year-round for breakfast, late May to mid-November for dinner; $$$$. Beach House Grill open mid-June to early September for breakfast, lunch, and dinner; $-$$. (www.chathambarsinn.com)

The Captain's House Inn of Chatham, 369-377 Old Harbor Rd., Chatham, MA 02633. 800-315-0728, 508-945-0127. Estatelike grounds, four-star amenities, and full concierge service will remind you of a European country hotel. The 19 rooms are divided among the 1839 white Greek Revival inn, a 200-year-old cottage, a carriage house, and a new building with double whirlpool baths. Open year-round. Breakfast included. $115-$325. (www.captainshouseinn.com)

Port Fortune Inn, 201 Main St., Chatham, MA 02633. 800-750-0792, 508-945-0792. Two turn-of-the-century cedar-shingle Cape Cod traditionals on one acre punctuate historic Chatham Village. Fourteen rooms, most with four-poster beds and some with ocean views, are decorated with antiques. Beaches, restaurants, and shops are close by. Take a walk to scenic Lighthouse Beach. Open February 1-December 31. Continental breakfast included. $90-$170. (www.capecod.net/portfortune)

Wequassett Inn, Pleasant Bay, Chatham, Cape Cod, MA 02633. 800-225-7125, 508-432-5400. This 104-room resort overlooks Pleasant Bay and claims a pretty, white-sand beach for its guests. The list of amenities includes tennis courts, a 68-foot pool beside the ocean, sailing, complimentary transport to golf courses, babysitting, and boat rentals. For a big-beach fix, the inn ferries guests to a quiet section of the Cape Cod National Seashore. You won't find a more attentive staff anywhere. Open April-November. $100-$510. Light snacks and cocktails served poolside. Eben Ryder House open mid-April to mid-November for lunch and dinner. $$$. (www.wequassett.com)

Where to Eat

Christian's, 443 Main St., Chatham. 508-945-3362. This is an upstairs-downstairs place. Locals frequent the upstairs restaurant, which is more casual. You can get the same menu as downstairs (more formal atmosphere) plus burgers and pizza and eat in a pub-style environment. Upstairs open year-round for lunch and dinner. Downstairs, where reservations are recommended, open mid-May to mid-October for dinner. $-$$$.

Chatham Wayside Inn, 512 Main St., Chatham. 800-391-5734 (for room reservations), 508-945-5550 (restaurant). The inn has 56 rooms, all with private baths. $95-$325. In the summer you can eat at the restaurant under the awning streetside, or year-round the cozy dining room welcomes hungry crowds. The menu includes seafood, pasta, rack of lamb, and steaks. This restaurant is popular among locals and visitors. Open year-round for breakfast, lunch, and dinner. $-$$$. (www.waysideinn.com)

What to See

Monomoy National Wildlife Refuge, Wikis Way off Morris Island Rd., Chatham. 508-945-0594. Monomoy's two barrier islands, North Monomoy and South Monomoy, are totally wild and unspoiled, accessible only by boat. Refuge tours available through the Cape Cod Museum of Natural History (508-896-3867) or Wellfleet Bay Wildlife Sanctuary (508-349-2615).

The Chatham Light. Few spots on the East Coast are equal to the view at "the Light." Drive down Main Street to the lighthouse and park for a spell. The light was built in 1828, then rebuilt 48 years later.

Band Concerts, Kate Gould Park, Main St., Chatham. Bring a blanket and a folding chair for music, dancing, community singing, and the colorfully uniformed 40-piece "house" band. Performances July-Labor Day, Friday 8 P.M. If weather is iffy, call the town offices, 508-945-5100, to confirm.

One Crazy Day on Martha's Vineyard

WE'VE ALWAYS HAD OUR SHARE OF VISITORS, BUT Martha's Vineyard was still a decently kept secret, at least on a national and international level. Then President Clinton chose the Vineyard for his vacation. Soon it seemed as if everyone was here. Every day I'd read in *The Boston Globe* about another celebrity arriving. I saw the Vineyard in all the big magazines.

So why would anyone, especially anyone who likes the feeling of discovering a place, want to come to the Vineyard? I still find my Vineyard mostly unchanged. Most places I go are no more crowded than usual (some crowds are good) and some are almost desolate (just don't expect to sail into a popular restaurant without a reservation).

Here are some of my favorite things to do. You could do most of them in 24 hours — but we don't recommend it. The *Vineyard Gazette* comes out on Friday and holds the key to one of the week's most anticipated events: yard sales. They're unrivaled here. Take a map and number the yard sales on a list in order based on proximity, opening times, and the desirability of goods.

My neighbor Alison Shaw, an earlier riser than we (at least on estate-sale days), roars past our house some Saturdays at 7:00 A.M. Alison works backward from Chilmark, heading first to the Chilmark Flea Market (Wednesday and Saturday), which opens at 8:30. Artisans sell Calder-like mobiles, hand-crafted furniture, and more. From there Alison motors down to the farmer's market at the old West Tisbury Agricultural Hall. "By arriving at nine," she instructs, "you get first pick of the wildflowers, and most important, you can get a good place in line at the Vietnamese cold-roll booth." We go to pick up fresh field greens for dinner salad, fresh-baked bread, buckets of wildflowers, biscotti for the baby, and jars of honey

Vineyard Haven Harbor boasts the most wooden boats of any small harbor in New England. (photo by Jim McElholm, courtesy Martha's Vineyard Chamber of Commerce)

made by the Dunkles, a local Chilmark clan. And celebrity watching is rewarding, if you like that sort of thing. Locals will never admit this — we like to say we just "let our celebrities go about their way," though most of us trade notes on whom we've seen standing eating at Red Cat (Kevin Costner) or trying to catch a ferry (Robert Redford).

Rainy-Day Amusements

Though the Vineyard is best on a breezy summer day, locals know how not to let the rain spoil the fun. The Vineyard Museum in Edgartown shows off whaling history and also features details from artist Thomas Hart Benton's famous murals painted for the WPA in the 1930s. Benton, a summer resident of Chilmark for 50 years, used a Chilmark family to model for the murals, which eventually graced public buildings all over the Midwest. Housed in a 12-room Colonial, the museum is also home to a world-famous, two-story Fresnel lens once located in the Gay Head lighthouse. You can hear voices from the island's past — over 250 older residents have recorded thoughts for you to listen to in the Oral History Center.

If the rain is still coming down, visit the Book Den East in Oak Bluffs, the kind of place that could make you look forward to rainy days. This two-story barn is filled with old maps, rare first editions, and good cheap paperbacks for the beach — after all, the sun can't hide forever.

Vineyard Museum, corner of Cooke and School sts., Edgartown. 508-627-4441. In summer Tuesday-Saturday 10- 5; in fall Wednesday-Friday 1-4 P.M., Saturday 10-4. $6, children 6-15 $4, under 6 free.

Book Den East, New York Ave., Oak Bluffs. 508-693-3946. Open June-Columbus Day Monday-Saturday 10-5, Sunday 1-5 P.M. Winter hours vary.

By noon Alison is racing down the street to Alley's General Store, a classic bit of Americana, for a muffin tin or wooden-handled scrub brushes before hitting the last yard sales. She tells me "you haven't lived" until you've eaten the doughnuts at Humphrey's — the real name is the Vineyard Foodshop in North Tisbury. "The place hasn't changed in 30 years," she says. "And neither has the doughnut recipe. Since the doughnuts are cooked in small batches all morning, you'll always find them piping hot. Definitely get more than one," she warns. "You'll finish the first one before you're out the front door." (I've concluded that the only way Alison stays so thin after all these spring rolls and doughnuts is by carrying all her yard-sale loot from her truck to her house every Saturday.)

At our house, after unloading our own loot, my family and I pack a picnic — from the farmer's market, or gourmet fare from the Vineyard Gourmet in Vineyard Haven, or Soigne in Edgartown — and head for the beach. We have several favorites depending on mood (and time of day):

Convivial mood: Try the Inkwell in Oak Bluffs, right on Seaview Avenue. Called this because of the black families (Oak Bluffs was the first black resort in America) who gather here, the Inkwell has the cozy, familiar feeling of a club beach — you see the same people every day. Mothers dangle their babies' toes in gentle surf. Families sit on big blankets for the whole day, playing card games, listening to jazz, reading. People meander among blankets, commenting on how much the kids have grown in a year.

Robinson Crusoe mood: Here's a good investment. Buy a pass for the Trustees of Reservations beaches and head to Chappaquiddick. Our favorite beach is at Wasque (East Beach is also spectacular), where you can fish, walk for miles, and see only a few other people. Another beloved Trustees beach is Long Point Wildlife Refuge in West Tisbury.

Town-beach mood: Menemsha town beach is mostly local families. The water is cooler here than on the Gulf Stream-warmed south shore or the practically tropical Vineyard

Sound side. There's a lifeguard and piers to walk along, from which you can admire yachts and sailboats and the Vineyard's fishing fleet. Menemsha Harbor, setting of the movie *Jaws* (until a few years ago, one of the shacks still had "Quint — Boat for Charter" painted on the door) is one of the prettiest in New England. There's a little store with good beach food, bathhouses with showers, a few shops up the road, and great fishing at the Menemsha Bight. Right across the bight is Lobsterville Beach, another gem (great fishing) in the town of Gay Head. So near — across 100 feet of swiftly moving water — and yet so far: about an hour's bike ride. But Hugh Taylor has solved this problem with his bike ferry, which crosses from Menemsha over to Lobsterville for $4 (one way). The sun sets right into the water at Menemsha — one of the few places where you can see that on the East Coast — and everyone claps as it drops below the horizon.

For dinner, it's a treat to do L'Étoile or Savoir Fare in

Edgartown, or Lola's in Oak Bluffs, or Le Grenier in Vineyard Haven, but here's what we do for just regular treats. With a bottle of wine we head up to Menemsha to the Home Port. This is a Vineyard institution: great seafood with views of the Menemsha Bight and sunset. But the dining room is busy. We go around to the screen door of the kitchen

The centerpiece of Ocean Park is the Oak Bluffs gazebo, which doubles as a bandstand for summer concerts. (photo by Jim McElhom, courtesy Martha's Vineyard Chamber of Commerce)

and order right there (the food is less than half the price of that inside — try the stuffed quahogs and the grilled bluefish). Then you can eat on the terrace (same sunset). This used to be a big secret; now it's only a medium-size secret, and who knows now after publishing this? So you may need to wait for a terrace table. Or take your meal and go sit on the docks or the beach.

At the end of our day, we take the babies to the band concerts in Ocean Park in Oak Bluffs and march them around with all the other kids in their pajamas. Then we walk home, looking for fireflies, and hit the sack early, hoping to someday beat Alison to a yard sale.

– Jamie Kageleiry

Editors' Picks for Martha's Vineyard

General Information

Vineyard Chamber of Commerce, Beach Rd., Vineyard Haven, MA 02568. 508-693-0085. (www.mvy.com)

Ferries: You need one to get here. Steamship Authority ferries take cars and depart from Woods Hole; 508-477-8600. Reservations strongly suggested. *Island Queen* departs Falmouth; 508-548-4800.

Hy-Line departs Hyannis; 508-775-7185. *Schamonchi* departs New Bedford; 508-997-1688. Or you can fly into the Vineyard Airport; 508-693-7022.

The Trustees of Reservations, at the Wakeman Center on Helen Ave., P.O. Box 2106, Vineyard Haven, MA 02568. 508-693-7662. Family memberships to all the Trustees properties in Massachusetts ($60) are good for a year and are available through the mail, at the Martha's Vineyard office, or at the gatehouse on each property. Gatehouses are open June 15-September 15, daily 9-5. Office is open year-round 9-5. (www.vineyard.net/org/trustees)

Where to Stay

Samoset on the Sound, Box 847, Seaview and Samoset aves., Oak Bluffs, MA 02557. 508-693-5148. This inn with seven rooms has two rooms overlooking the beach, one with a private deck. Open late May to mid-October. $60-$150.

The Oak House, Box 299, Seaview Ave., Oak Bluffs, MA 02557. 800-245-5979, 508-693-4187. This fancy 1872 Victorian was built for Massachusetts Governor Claflin. Named for the oak paneling throughout 10 island-themed rooms, the house is furnished with antiques. Each room has a private bath, and some also have a porch. Open mid-May to mid-October. Continental breakfast and afternoon tea included. $110-$260. (www.vineyard.net/inns/oakhouse)

Outermost Inn, Lighthouse Rd., Gay Head, MA 02535. 508-645-3511. The inn's six rooms and one suite are outfitted with natural fabrics, neutral colors, and unfinished furniture, letting the spectacular ocean views take the limelight. Owned by Hugh and Jeanne Taylor, the common rooms are filled with musical instruments. Open May-October. Full breakfast included. $180-$320. Dining room serves fixed-price dinner. Reservations required. $$$$. (www.outermostinn.com)

Menemsha Inn and Cottages, North Rd. (Chilmark), P.O. Box 38C, Menemsha, MA 02552. 508-645-2521. Choose from six luxury suites in the carriage house, nine rooms in the main house, or 12 housekeeping cottages. The latter feature porches, kitchens, outdoor showers, private baths, and fireplaces. Beach passes included. Open May-early November. Continental breakfast included. Rooms $125-$140, suites $180, cottages $750-$1475 weekly. (www.vineyard.net/biz/menemshainn)

Where to Eat

L'Étoile, in the Charlotte Inn, 27 South Summer St., Edgartown. 508-627-5187. Eat in the garden surrounded by brick walls. The price is tall, but worth every penny. Open in summer nightly, call for off-season schedule. Fixed price four-course dinner $68. Reservations recommended. $$$$.

Savoir Fare, Old Post Office Sq., Edgartown. 508-627-9864. Our Vineyard correspondent writes, "Ate here a few weeks ago and it was great, great, great. . . . Instead of an entrée, we tried a bunch of appetizers along with a few unique and scrumptious salads." Open in July and August nightly for dinner; April-October Thursday-Sunday. $$$$.

Lola's, Beach Rd., Oak Bluffs. 508-693-5007. A colorful mural composed of local faces serves as the perfect backdrop for the seafood served up Southern style at the newest place to "see and be seen." The gospel brunch on Sundays is not to be missed. Open year-round for dinner, Sunday 10-2 for brunch. $$$-$$$$.

Le Grenier, 82 Main St., Vineyard Haven. 508-693-4906. Traditional French food prepared by Jean Dupon never disappoints, from frogs' legs to bouillabaisse. Bring your own spirits. Open year-round for dinner. $$$-$$$$.

Home Port, North Rd., Menemsha. 508-645-2679. This popular seafood restaurant fills by early evening, so locals head to the back kitchen door and order there, where grilled bluefish and other favorites (try the stuffed quahogs) are about half the price. Bring your own spirits. Open May 1 to mid-October nightly for dinner. Reservations required. $$$-$$$$.

What to See

The Farmer's Market, Old Agricultural Hall, State Rd., West Tisbury. A Vineyard tradition. Open mid-June to mid-October Saturday 9-noon; June-August also Wednesday 2:30-5:30 P.M.

Chicama Vineyards, Stoney Hill Rd., West Tisbury. 888-244-2262, 508-693-0309. Tour the oldest winery in the state. In addition to the wines, shop for herb vinegars, mustards, dressings, and jams. Open year-round. Tours late May to mid-October Monday-Saturday 11-5, Sunday 1-5 P.M.; call for other times.

The Granary Gallery at the Red Barn Emporium, Old County Rd., West Tisbury. 800-472-6279, 508-693-0455. You'll find folk art, landscape paintings, and photography here. Open late May to mid-October daily 10-5 or by appointment. (www.granarygallery.com)

The Field Gallery & Sculpture Garden, State Rd., West Tisbury Center. 508-693-5595. You'll know you are in the right place when you see the dancing white figures. Open May-September daily 10-5; off-season weekends only. Artist receptions some Sundays June-September 5-7 P.M.

The Perfect College Town: Williamstown

Tucked in the Hills of Western Massachusetts

TWO DAYS STAND OUT AMONG ALL OTHERS: THE first was the hot, inglorious day I arrived on campus, amid the flat green of late August. I was 18, and the only thing I noticed about the mountains was the nausea and dread they inspired as the family van wound up and down the hills toward Williams College. I was too busy that day shaking hands and trying to sound as if I belonged there to notice the trees. The second day was the day I graduated.

In between I spent four years at Williams College in Williamstown, Massachusetts. These four years of learning and growing ended just recently, and I am still adjusting to the change of scenery. I have exchanged the snug vistas of the Purple Valley for the more imposing, singular views of Mount Monadnock in southern New Hampshire. It has been ridiculously difficult to leave Williamstown. Especially after the trick it pulled on the departing seniors.

It was mid-May. The air was thick with the heady sweetness of lilacs in full, unprecedented bloom. They simply stunned us all. No one could remember the lilacs as ever having been quite so beautiful. As they brazenly bloomed on for weeks, they became ever more unavoidable and impossibly lovely. All my other years here, I had barely noticed the bushes all around me. Now they were suddenly sporting fragrant, deep-purple bundles, blinding white tassels — even some practically azure bouquets. I found my friends up to their necks — sometimes their waists — in the bushes laden with weighty blooms. These blossoms had succeeded in stopping my studious classmates from buzzing over Route 2, intent on errands and worries, and infused a little perspective into the atmosphere of a college town in spring. All of us now were slowed by flowers. Then, of course, they gave us diplomas and made us leave.

Other than this unexpected infatuation with the lilacs, I had spent my Williamstown years looking down: at books, at projects, doggedly tracing my paths between work in the dining hall, classes, and friends. During my last few weeks there, however, I found myself looking up a lot more than looking down.

I finally began to notice the skyline; I was eager to impress all of its details upon my memory. The cupolas, church steeples, towers, and weather vanes of the buildings had never held such import before. Each song pealing from the bells of Thompson Memorial Chapel — everything from "Oklahoma" to "Puff the Magic Dragon" — made me smile. I envied the bell-ringing students whose job was sweetened by the carte-blanche policy concerning their music selections. As long as they could arrange it for the bells, they could play it and impose any mood they wished on the captive Williams community.

And captive we were. For much of my four years, I stayed right in Williamstown. Friends who chose metropolitan schools always wondered at how I could be happy in such an isolated and pastoral place. Someone with presence of mind might have refuted with Henry David Thoreau's summation of Williams: "It would be of no small advantage if every college were thus located at the base of a mountain." Although Williamstown may seem small to some — boxed in, even, by its scenery — there was never a sense of being limited here. Yes, my dorm rooms were staggeringly small, yet they always held a view of the mountains. Though I spent my college years in the depths of a valley, I always knew I was preparing for what lay over those hills.

I won't deny that there were nights, long nights of studying, especially in winter, when Williamstown seemed isolated and even lonely. And I didn't have time to fully ex-

WHAT THE LOCALS KNOW

The Perfect View of Williamstown

Blair walk (or drive) is five miles. If you're walking, leave your car in the public parking lot at the foot of Spring Street. Follow Spring as it curves off to the left past the Towne Field House and Weston Field. Take the first right onto Meacham Street. Follow the curve of Meacham past the Taconic Golf Club. Go right onto Water Street and follow it for 1.5 miles, then take the left onto Blair Road. This gravel road will take you to the best, most satisfying view to be had of Williamstown's skyline and the glories of the Purple Valley. Be sure to pause at the apex of the walk before you plunge back toward town. Follow the hilly road until you reach the intersection of Blair and Stratton roads. Take a left, which will bring you back to Williamstown along busy Route 2.

plore what it had to offer. I never stood on the top of Mount Greylock, where Herman Melville and Nathaniel Hawthorne once picnicked. I never saw the display of the founding documents of the United States at the Chapin Library of Rare Books. I lived a few houses down from the Sterling and Francine Clark Art Institute and couldn't visit as often as I would have liked.

It was the everyday wealth of Williamstown that I sought out: the luxury of being able to walk down to Spring Street between classes and pick up the necessities, such as coffee (breakfast) at Cold Spring Coffee Roasters, cookies (lunch) at Suchèle Bakers, and gifts and cards at Library An-

College students Steven Ehrenberg and Cate Williams enjoy a stroll outside Stetson Hall at Williams College.
(photo by Bob Krist, courtesy Williams College)

tiques. I appreciated the luxury of recognizing every face I saw as I crossed Route 2, which neatly bisects the campus between the sciences and the humanities. These were faces that had come from all around the world to be here, in this valley.

When I needed a break from my studies, there was always Images Cinema to the rescue with a worthwhile film, followed by an Orange Raz smoothie at Lickety-Split. When an essay was giving me trouble, I strolled up to the Clark to search the enigmatic expression of Degas's sculptural masterpiece, *Little Dancer Aged Fourteen*. There were the planetarium shows in the Old Hopkins Observatory, too. It was built in the 1830s by Professor Albert Hopkins and his students. They quarried the native stone themselves and constructed what is now the oldest extant observatory in the United States. Once the vaulted ceiling of the planetarium was painted blue, spangled with gold stars painted in groups to form constellations. Those astral configurations have since been painted over, but they served as a reminder to me that more looking up was in order.

On graduation day, I took a walk by myself to escape the crowds of well-wishers. I needed to look at something that would make more sense than the obscure Latin on my diploma. I headed south along the Green River on Water Street, a long, slow pilgrimage that would bring me to the ultimate view of what I was leaving behind.

At the apex of Blair Road, I stood in the shadow of Mount Prospect and took it all in one last time. The lush, rolling green of the Taconic hills, the levels of wooded fields thrown into rich relief by a setting sun, and the spires of Williamstown's skyline nestled among it all. And I knew this was the closest I could get to being blessed by a place.

I wonder if I will find such an absolutely satisfying prospect here in my new home. For now, I will close my eyes, remember the scent of lilacs so thick in the air that it actually felt like a new element being discovered, and imagine the dusky perfection of Williamstown in spring.

– Erica Bollerud

Editors' Picks for
Williamstown

General Information

Williamstown Chamber of Commerce, P.O. Box 357, Williamstown, MA 01267. Information booth at junction of rtes. 7 and 2 near the rotary. 800-214-3799.

Where to Stay

Friendly note of warning: don't even try to get a room in early June. Parents reserve accommodations four years in advance in anticipation of graduation. (To avoid the frenzy, come in spring, and catch the lilacs.)

Field Farm Guest House, 554 Sloan Rd., Williamstown, MA 01267. 413-458-3135. This intimate house, surrounded by 296 acres of protected farmland, is filled with modern art and 1950s-style Danish modern furnishings. It offers five guest rooms, all with private baths. Use of miles of hiking trails, tennis courts, and a swimming pool. Open year-round. Full breakfast included. $125.

Steep Acres Farm B&B, 520 White Oaks Rd., Williamstown, MA 01267. 413-458-3774. Four country cottages, circa 1900, with spectacular views of the Berkshire hills and Green Mountains. Open year-round. Breakfast included. $85.

River Bend Farm, 643 Simonds Rd. (Rte. 7N), Williamstown, MA 01267. 413-458-3121. 1770 Georgian Colonial, with four antiques-filled rooms, surrounded by gardens. Open April-October. Breakfast included. $90.

Where to Eat

Cold Spring Coffee Roasters, Ltd., 47 Spring St., Williamstown. 413-458-5010. Fuel up and go, or laze on the stools in the front window for some prime people-watching. Open daily 7-6. $.

Suchèle Bakers, 37 Spring St., Williamstown. 413-458-2251. The place to stop for comfort food during a day of sightseeing (or exam week). Open Tuesday-Saturday 7-5. $.

Lickety-Split, 69 Spring St., Williamstown. 413-458-1818. Stop by for some Herrell's ice cream, a fruit smoothie, or lunch. They've got soups, quiche, salads, and sandwiches. Or skip lunch and have more ice cream. Open on the terrace in the summer daily 11:30-11; hours vary during the rest of the year.

Pappa Charlie's Deli, 28 Spring St., Williamstown. 413-458-5969. Probably the closest you'll ever get to eating Eric Stoltz. This laid-back eatery offers huge deli sandwiches concocted to evoke their namesake celebrities. The cranberry sauce and turkey of the Richard Chamberlain on wheat runs neck-and-neck with the roasted vegetables in the Bo Derek pita for my favorite. Open during the summer Monday-Saturday 8 A.M.-11 P.M., Sunday 9-9. Open the rest of the year Monday-Thursday 8 A.M.-9 P.M., Friday and Saturday 8 A.M.-11 P.M., Sunday 9-9. $.

Main Street Café, 16 Water St., Williamstown. 413-458-3210. Its recent move from North Bennington certainly hasn't affected the excellent quality of its cuisine. Choose between its fine dining and bistro menus. The bistro offers salads, seafoods, and oven-baked pizza, while the fine dining menu offers impeccable pasta and seafood specialties, such as wok-seared shrimp sautéed in garlic sauce with fresh herbs and plum tomatoes over linguine, cooked to order. Open daily for lunch and dinner. Reservations recommended. $$-$$$$.

What to See

Chapin Library of Rare Books, Stetson Hall, Williams College, Williamstown. 413-597-2462. Original printings of the Declaration of Independence, Articles of Confederation, Constitution, Bill of Rights, and George Washington's copy of the Federalist Papers are on permanent display. Special exhibits vary. Open Monday-Friday 10 A.M.-noon, 1-5 P.M. Free.

Sterling and Francine Clark Art Institute, 225 South St., Williamstown. 413-458-9545. A rich collection of works by French impressionists, American masters, and others, safely secreted in the Berkshires. Open July-August daily 10-5, Tuesdays 10-8; September-June Tuesday-Sunday 10-5. Admission July-October $5; members, students, children free. Everyone free Tuesday. Free every day November-June. (www.clark.williams.edu)

Milham Planetarium, Old Hopkins Observatory, Main St., Williamstown. 413-597-2188. Topics of these student-run shows vary seasonally. Shows during the summer, Tuesday and Thursday 8 P.M., Fridays at 7 P.M. the rest of the year. Reservations a must. Free.

Williamstown Theatre Festival, Adams Memorial Theatre, Main St., Williamstown. Box office 413-597-3400. The stars alight in the Purple Valley. You may find yourself directing certain luminaries of the stage toward the nearest ATM (I did when I showed Austin Pendleton where to get his cash last summer). Acclaimed ten-week, ten-play summer festival of classic and new plays, countless readings and workshops.

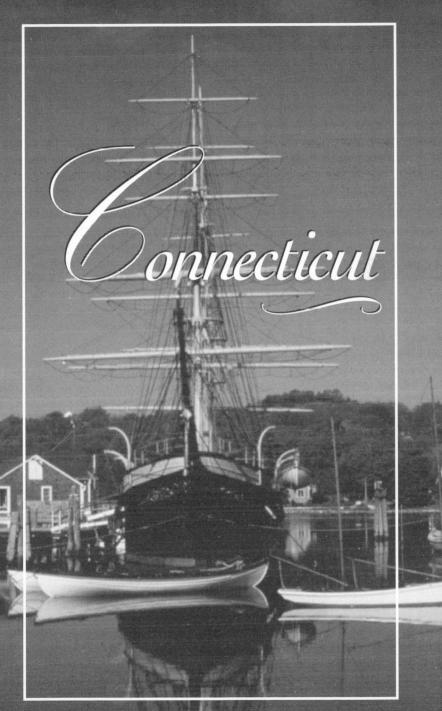

Connecticut

Square-rigger **Joseph Conrad** *at Mystic Seaport.*
(courtesy Mystic Seaport)

Keeper of Memories in Hartford, a City of Legends

ALL RIGHT, TRUTH: GROWING UP IN A CITY CONSID-
erably west of the Hudson, I'd formed a picture of New England by the age of ten, cobbled together from a visit to Old Sturbridge Village, a walk along the Freedom Trail in Boston, images of pilgrims, turkeys, Plymouth Rock, and a family vacation to the White Mountains.

Drawn to an idea as much as a place, I eventually made my way to Vermont and by the age of 20 had become a champion of country life. I did chores for a Vermont farmer and photographed the same cows in the same place that in-

WHAT THE LOCALS KNOW

Ten Things Not to Miss in Hartford

Before becoming executive director of the Antiquarian & Landmarks Society, Bill Hosley spent 17 years as curator of American Decorative Arts at the Wadsworth Atheneum. He is a longtime Connecticut resident who knows and loves Hartford better than anyone we know. Everyone who gets within 100 miles of Hartford knows about the Mark Twain House, the Harriet Beecher Stowe House, and the Old State House, but Bill notes that there are many other heritage treasures as fascinating but less well known. Here is his list (in his words) of the top ten things not to miss.

1. Butler-McCook Homestead, a preserved (not restored) house that exhibits four generations of family life on Main Street and remains Hartford's best Colonial-era house with the oldest intact collection of art and antiques.

2. Connecticut State Capitol, a gilded-age spectacle with all the Victorian bells and whistles.

3. Soldiers and Sailors Memorial Arch: Almost every town and city in New England has a Civil War monument. For beauty, power, and raw emotion, Hartford's Soldiers and Sailors rules!

4. Museum of Connecticut History: From the Charter Oak to the Hall of Connecticut inventions, this is a must-see treasure box.

5. Cedar Hill Cemetery, designed by Swiss landscape architect Jacob Weidenmann: Consider this an outdoor museum of art, botany, history, and the final resting place of J. P. Morgan, Sam and Elizabeth Colt, and other local dignitaries.

6. The Connecticut Historical Society, collecting for more than a century and a half: The CHS helped create the American antiques scene as we know it and today houses Connecticut furniture, clocks, and treasures galore. *(continued)*

(continued from previous page)

7. The Wallace Nutting Collection, America's biggest and best collection of Pilgrim treasures, assembled by the famous photographer and champion of New England country life.

8. Daniel Wadsworth and the Hudson River School: Wadsworth made history by introducing Frederic Church to Thomas Cole and eventually amassed one of the first great collections of American paintings.

9. A Connecticut Furniture Treasury, from the Wetmore Parlor, America's best 18th-century painted parlor and the masterpieces of the Chapin "school" of cabinetwork: There is no finer collection of its type in the country.

10. *Repentant Eve* **by Edward Bartholomew,** a Hartford native who made it big as a sculptor in Rome: No other artist has better captured the timeless emotion of Eve's grief.

Edward Bartholomew's **Repentant Eve** *can be seen in Morgan Great Hall at the Wadsworth Atheneum.*
(courtesy Wadsworth Atheneum)

spired Vermont artist Woody Jackson (and his coconspirators at Ben & Jerry's) to create one of the most durable images of Vermont today.

New England may be a rural idea, but I eventually reconnected the two halves of my life by discovering and learning to know and love New England cities. By and large, New Englanders got rich by inventing things, making things, selling things, marketing things, and taking risks. The big payouts came in New England's cities. And it was in building their cities that New Englanders explored the boundary between public virtue and private wealth. Cities like Hartford, Lowell, Bridgeport, and Worcester mostly survived the Depression, only to be strangled nearly to death in the 1950s and 1960s by a new army of highway engineers and urban planners, hell-bent on fixing something that was not quite broken. Rumor has it that New England's cities are now mostly in ruins. As Mark Twain said, "Rumors of their demise are greatly exaggerated."

A long tenure as a curator at Hartford's Wadsworth Atheneum taught me something special about New England cities and a few things about America's "oldest public art museum." However the Atheneum ranks among American art museums, it is surely the only one that started out life as something else. An atheneum, what is it? And what does it have to do with private wealth and public virtue?

Atheneums were a product of the Age of Andrew Jackson and Walt Whitman. Blustery, confident, and passionately democratic, they thrived from the 1830s through the Civil War, until the Gilded Age when art museums became all the rage. Until the 20th century, New England had more atheneums than art museums, with examples in Providence, Boston, and Portsmouth.

With their libraries and reading rooms, picture galleries and antiquarian relics, collections of natural specimens and public halls for visiting lecturers, atheneums were little public universities in miniature, designed for an age that had no truly public universities. Inspired by ancient

Greece, they were created to foster nothing less than competent, resourceful, and virtuous citizens. Life learning, self-improvement, a bedrock faith in the power of liberal learning, these were the pillars of the atheneum age.

So what is this Wadsworth Atheneum and how is it different from your typical art museum? To begin with, being 155-plus years old, it has forgotten more than most Ameri-

**A court cupboard from the Wallace Nutting
Collection at the Wadsworth Atheneum.**
(*courtesy Wadsworth Atheneum*)

can museums know. Its collections represent layer upon layer of public trust and private passion. Because it is more ancient than most, its storage vaults are haunted by memories and lined with treasures. It was there, on the walls but especially in the storage areas, that I discovered the personalities who built the city I love.

For most of its history, Wadsworth Athencum was little more and nothing less than an expression of public love by the men (and one great woman) whose names adorn its various buildings and galleries. Its founder, Daniel Wadsworth, so typified Connecticut habits and Connecticut virtues that his family was almost public property, a kind of Yankee royalty, beloved and ever present, but never quite touchable by mortal men. Father Jeremiah belonged to the generation of venerated worthies who won the War of Independence. George Washington was a guest in young Daniel's home and may have actually slept there!

In 1858, when celebrated artist and native son Edward Bartholomew died in Rome, Hartford's business leaders dispatched a local stonecutter named James Batterson to Italy to recover what remained of his sculpture studio. A year later Wadsworth Atheneum installed the collection as a shrine to the "genius" of Connecticut art. And young Batterson? He went on to become the president of the Atheneum's board of trustees, Hartford's first collector of Old Masters, and a renowned monument maker, whose work occupies prime positions in the National Cemeteries at both Gettysburg and Antietam battlefields. Along the way he also managed to found Travelers Insurance Company.

City builders weave in and out of the Atheneum's history, often leaving material evidence of their passions, travels, and accomplishments. Daniel Wadsworth ensured that the lessons of the Revolution were enshrined on the walls of the institution bearing his name by commissioning a set of artist John Trumbull's most famous history paintings, including the *Signing of the Declaration of Independence*, best known from the image on the back of the $10 bill.

The Gilded Age brought a new generation of leadership in the Reverend Francis Goodwin, whose mother was J. P. Morgan's sister and whose father, Major James, was the "insurance king of Hartford." Small world. Deep pockets. Big vision. The Reverend Francis transformed Wadsworth Atheneum into an art museum, helped fill the park across Main Street with statuary, and lobbied to build the deliciously high-Victorian Connecticut State Capitol in the 1870s. He built public parks and Victorian landmarks, left Wadsworth Atheneum with a handful of paintings and home furnishings, and prompted his Morgan cousins to build and furnish an addition that more than doubled its size.

At the age of 35, Elizabeth Hart Jarvis Colt, the widow of Sam Colt, the revolver king, inherited control over one of the first American industrial fortunes. Over the next 40 years, as the empress of Coltsville, she built legendary art collections, founded charities and institutions, and erected civic monuments and architectural jewels citywide. The Atheneum's Colt Memorial was the first wing of an American art museum to bear the name of a woman patron.

As the Wadsworth Atheneum resonates with civic pride and accomplishment, the city echoes back, providing a framework for the museum's collections. Poring over the museum's shelves of memories, I discovered the power of connecting collections with the world beyond the museum's doors. A visitor's experience is best when it neither begins nor ends at the museum threshold. It is the richness, variety, and yes, even the messiness of it all, that make New England cities like Hartford our new Egyptian tombs. Scrape off the dust, dig a little, reassemble the fragments, and you see something jewel-like and inspiring.

– William Hosley

Editors' Picks for Hartford and Simsbury

General Information

Greater Hartford Tourism District, 234 Murphy Rd., Hartford, CT 06114. 800-793-4480, 860-244-8181. (www.travelfile.com/get/ghtd)

Where to Stay

Goodwin Hotel, 1 Haynes St., Hartford, CT 06103. 800-922-5006, 860-246-7500. Located opposite the Civic Center, this is Hartford's luxury hotel, with 124 rooms and 11 suites, lounges, entertainment, health facilities, and parking. Open year-round. $79-$154. Elegant dining in Pierpont's. Open Monday-Friday for breakfast, lunch, and dinner, Saturday breakfast and dinner only, Sunday breakfast and brunch only. $-$$$. (www.goodwinhotel.com)

Simsbury 1820 House, 731 Hopmeadow St., Simsbury, CT 06070. 800-879-1820, 860-658-7658. An 1820 country manor on the National Register of Historic Places with leaded-glass windows, finely carved woodwork, elegant paintings, and fireplaces. The inn, with 32 rooms with private baths, overlooks the center of historic Simsbury. Open year-round. Continental breakfast included. $115-$185. 1820 House Café serves seasonal specialties using fresh local ingredients. Favorites include pasta and seafood dishes. Open Monday-Thursday for dinner. $-$$.

Old Babcock Tavern, 484 Mile Hill Rd. (Rte. 31), Tolland, CT 06084. 860-875-1239. This Colonial house was once a tavern and is listed on the National Register of Historic Places. Nicely restored with early paneling, exposed timbers, and four working fireplaces. It offers three rooms with private baths. Open year-round. Breakfast included, and there is always homemade pie or coffee cake. $70-$85.

Where to Eat

Max Downtown, 185 Asylum St., Hartford. 860-522-2530. Located in City Place, across from the Civic Center, this is one of three Max restaurants in the area. It is a featured chop house, with contemporary global cuisine serving a variety of steaks, veal chops, salmon, tuna, and sea bass. Open Monday-Friday for lunch, daily for dinner. $$$.

Peppercorn's Grill, 357 Main St., Hartford. 860-547-1714. Here you will find tasty pasta dishes as well as contemporary Italian fare including lobster ravioli, delicious veal entrées, and pizzas. Open Monday-Friday for lunch; Monday-Saturday for dinner. $$.

Museum Café at the Wadsworth Atheneum, 600 Main St., Hartford. 860-728-5989. This newly renovated café is just what you need after a day of museum going. Enjoy soups, salads, pasta, and interesting omelets. Open Tuesday-Sunday for lunch. $.

What to See

Butler-McCook Homestead, 396 Main St., Hartford. 860-247-8996. Open May 15-October 15, Tuesday, Thursday, Sunday noon-4. $4, children 18 and under $1.

Connecticut State Capitol, Capitol Ave. at Trinity St., Hartford. 860-240-0222. Open for tours April-October Monday-Friday 9-3, Saturday 10:15-2:15. Free.

Soldiers and Sailors Memorial Arch, Bushnell Park, one block west of Main St., at Gold and Jewel sts., Hartford. 860-232-6710. The park is open year-round daily. Memorial Arch and Park Tree tours May-October, Thursday, every 10 minutes 11:30-1:30. Free. (www.bushnellpark.org)

Museum of Connecticut History, Connecticut State Library (across from State Capitol), 231 Capitol Ave., Hartford. 860-566-3056. Open year-round Monday-Friday 9:30-4. Free.

Cedar Hill Cemetery, 253 Fairfield Ave., Hartford. 860-956-3311. Open year-round November-March daily 7-5, April-October daily 7 A.M.-8 P.M. Call to arrange for a tour. Topics, ranging from monumental architecture and landscaping to bird-watching to local historical figures, vary monthly. Free.

The Connecticut Historical Society, 1 Elizabeth St., Hartford. 860-236-5621. Open year-round. Museum open Tuesday-Sunday noon-5. Library open Tuesday-Saturday 10-5. Museum and library admission fees: $6, seniors $5, students $3, members and age 5 and under free. (www.hartnet.org/~chs)

Wadsworth Atheneum, 600 Main St., Hartford. 860-278-2670. The nation's oldest public art museum, with over 50,000 works spanning 5,000 years, including Renaissance and baroque paintings, decorative arts, costumes and textiles, Hudson River School paintings, impressionist masters, African-American art, 20th-century paintings and sculpture. Open year-round Tuesday-Sunday 11-5, open first Thursday of select months until 8 P.M.; closed Monday and major holidays. $7, seniors and students $5, children 6-17 $3, under 6 free (free on Thursday and before noon on Saturday). (www.hartnet.org/~wadsworth)

There's Nothing Like the Brooklyn Fair

An Agricultural Tradition in Connecticut's Northeast Corner

MOST OF THE YEAR THE SMALL TOWN OF BROOKLYN HAS ABOUT 6,500 people nestled in the gently rolling hills of northeast Connecticut, the so-called "Quiet Corner" of the state. But for the four days that the Brooklyn Agricultural Fair is in operation over the last weekend of August, thousands of cars fill the village's hayfields and back lanes, and some 115,000 souls disembark to watch magnificent draft horses or to nuzzle a prize Hampshire sheep; to toss a ring for an overstuffed pink boa or to eat Troop 44's great chicken barbecue.

For the most part, Brooklynites accept the bother that comes with the fair good-naturedly. Even those few who admit they are annoyed by the annual disruption of life say they understand that it's what keeps the shine on the new fire truck, which the fair's revenue helped the town purchase a few years back. But more important, the fair is also part of their heritage.

Dating from 1824, the Brooklyn Fair bills itself as the nation's oldest continuously operating agricultural fair. There may be fairs that have been around longer in total number of years, points out Don Francis, first selectman and former president of the Windham County Agricultural Society, "but we've run this thing straight since 1851, through wind and rain, heat and drought and hurricane." The Pomfret Agricultural Society, he explains, the forerunner of today's Windham Society, mounted its first exhibition of cattle and sheep in 1820. The fair eventually relocated to a pasture near the heart of Brooklyn and has been there ever since.

Animal demonstrations and displays are the calling card of the Brooklyn Agricultural Fair. (photo by Neil Delmonico, courtesy Northeast Connecticut Visitors District)

When Francis started as county agricultural agent back in the 1950s, there were more than 1,300 poultry and 800 working dairy farms in Windham County; by 1980 those figures were down to 50 and 100 respectively. Agriculture, in short, was following the same path to extinction that area textile mills had traveled 50 years earlier. The nature of the fair was also threatened. Amusement companies offered to double the amount of revenue generated if the fair organizers agreed to nix the animal competitions, tractor pulls, and beehive exhibits.

No deal. Says Francis: "Basically we lose money on our agricultural exhibits and programs, but we increased our commitment to them because they represent our heritage, our cultural legacy. We built a new animal exhibition hall and expanded the classes of competition. We even added a mule show."

Today you'd have trouble finding a more impressive assemblage of sheep, cattle, goats, pigs, draft horses, chickens,

---

The Other Incredibly Clever Martha

Martha Gummersall-Paul has been living in the Quiet Corner for 11 years and for all that time has been impressing locals with her gardens. Anything you'd ever want to know about herbs, Martha can tell you. Her shop, Martha's Herbary, is a must for any gardener. Here you will find unusual garden accessories, books, wreaths, unique herbs and specialty plants, demonstration gardens, raised beds of culinary herbs, and a beautiful sunken garden of medicinal herbs. Martha conducts cooking classes emphasizing the use of fresh herbs; here you can learn to make herb-flavored mustards, vinegars, and other great kitchen gifts.

Martha's Herbary, 589 Pomfret St., Pomfret. 860-928-0009. Open daily 10-5. (www.marthasherbary.com)

and birds of every feather. Teamsters come from all over New England to compete in Brooklyn's ox pulls and draft-horse shows, and the fair maintains the last harness race in Connecticut. "We are determined to keep this thing special," says Francis. "We think this is what a fair ought to be."

Wherever you turn in Brooklyn, you are reminded of the way things ought to be. Brooklyn has managed to preserve the classic look of a New England town in the face of rampant development elsewhere. Home to some of the finest Greek Revival architecture in America and the oldest Episcopal church in Connecticut, its redbrick jailhouse, still functioning as a state lockup, is on the National Register of Historic Places.

Beverly and Charles Yates were drawn to Brooklyn by its authenticity. They live and run a B&B in a stately old Colonial they call Friendship Valley. The Yateses love to share the interesting history of their house, which was once the home of George Benson, a Quaker abolitionist who sheltered Prudence Crandall from state and federal authorities prior to the Civil War. Crandall was the Canterbury woman who was tried in the Windham County Courthouse (now Brooklyn's town hall) in 1845 for the crime of "educating young Negro girls" in her home. Benson's daughter Helen married firebrand abolitionist William Lloyd Garrison in the front parlor of Friendship Valley.

On the same afternoon that teenage lovers were screaming their lungs out on the Tilt-a-Whirl at the Brooklyn Fair, Richard Booth, a retired biology professor at Central Connecticut State College, was visiting the Old Trinity Church. He is the church's caretaker and de facto historian, who says the old church holds services only once a year — on All Saints' Sunday — but that it remains one of the most visited and photographed churches in New England. It was built in 1771 by Godfrey Malbone, a land-rich Tory from Newport, Rhode Island, whose running feud with Israel Putnam is the stuff of local legend. Malbone is said to have built the Episcopal church to defy Israel Putnam, local Revolutionary War hero, and other patriots who tried to assess him £200 to help pay for a new Congregational church. "Both churches were eventually built," says Booth. "Israel Putnam was originally the sexton of the Congregational church, but the Putnams eventually came up here to Trinity Church — that's why they are now buried all over the burying ground." The Putnams and the Malbones eventually intermarried, ending the feud.

Bob and Jimmie Booth's Golden Lamb Buttery is as much an eccentric symbol of Brooklyn's old-fashioned values as Trinity Church or the fair. The restaurant is in a beautiful barn set on a 1,000-acre farm. You have to know how to get there, locals like to say, to get there.

Dining at the Buttery is a full evening affair — and an experience critics have raved about for almost 30 years. It has never advertised, yet reservations for its two nightly seatings are booked sometimes a year in advance. Predinner cocktails usually move from the barn's porch — with its vista of rolling hayfields, pond, and forests — to the back of a hay wagon, where guests sip wine and enjoy a serenade from a local folk songstress, while Bob, a stout, puckish, pearl-haired man beneath a signature white pith helmet, guides the entourage around part of the working farm where his parents once made exquisite wool. It's delightful hokum.

It seems to rub off. On the same night the "Amazing Castle Family" was doing its flashy song-and-dance routine down at the fairgrounds, you could also see a Buttery patron suddenly leap to his feet and belt out a Gershwin love song to his wife. It was an extraordinary moment; the 60-odd other diners applauded wildly.

"Does this happen here often?" a visitor asked Bob Booth. "All the time, like spontaneous combustion," he explained, smiling. "We hope that's because people feel really at home here. After all, it's our home. There's no place on earth lovelier than Brooklyn. We honestly believe this couldn't happen anyplace else."

– James Dodson

Editors' Picks for the Quiet Corner

General Information

Northeast Connecticut Visitors District, P.O. Box 598, Putnam, CT 06260. 888-628-1228, 860-928-1228. A comprehensive resource for travelers to the area, these folks provide an excellent *Getaway Guide* that offers everything from lodging, antiquing, shopping, and dining to camping and theater. Don't visit without this guide. (www.webtravels.com/quietcorner)

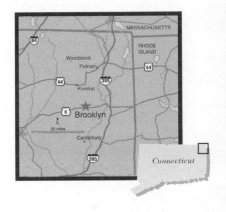

Where to Stay

Friendship Valley B&B Inn, 60 Pomfret Rd. (Rte. 169), P.O. Box 845, Brooklyn, CT 06234. 860-779-9696. Located in the National Historic District, this 18th-century house on scenic Route 169 is set on 12 wooded acres, with stone walls and picket fences. Each of the five guest rooms has private bath and antique furnishings. Hearty breakfasts are served on fine china in the dining room with fireplace or on the sunny breakfast porch. Open year-round. Includes breakfast. $85-$125.

Chickadee Cottage Bed & Breakfast, 375 Wrights Crossing Rd., P.O. Box 110, Pomfret, CT 06259. 860-963-0587. This lovely circa 1900 Cape was once part of a large estate. It is located on ten acres surrounded by extensive perennial gardens, furnished with antiques and traditional furniture, and has a sunroom, woodstove, fax machine, bicycles, and cat in residence. There are two rooms, each with private bath and cozy linens. Right across the street you'll find a 500-acre Audubon sanctuary with nature paths. Open year-round. Breakfast included. $75-$95. (www.webtravels.com/chickadeecottage)

Taylor's Corner B&B, 880 Rte. 171, Woodstock, CT 06281. 860-974-0490. A romantic, completely restored 18th-century Colonial on five acres, boasting eight working fireplaces (two with beehive ovens). The house, which has three guest rooms with private baths, is surrounded by English gardens, pastures, and towering trees and is furnished with antiques. The building is on the National Register of Historic Places. Open year-round. Breakfast included (full breakfast on weekends, continental weekdays). $70-$90. (www.neguide.com/taylors)

The Tolland Inn, 63 Tolland Green, Tolland, CT 06084. 860-872-0800. An 1800 Colonial inn on a historic village green. The building has exposed beams, a fireplace, sunporch, living room, common areas, and views of village green and gardens. The seven rooms all have private baths; and there is one room with fireplace and hot tub, one hottub suite, and one suite with a fireplace, queen canopy bed, and bay windows. Open year-round. Full breakfast included. $70-$130. (www.bbonline.com/ct/tollinn)

Where to Eat

Golden Lamb Buttery, 499 Wolf Den Rd. (off Rte. 169), Brooklyn. 860-774-4423. You gotta love a place that serves "hash" for lunch, made out of chateaubriand. And if the place is a barn that overlooks a 20-acre pond on a 1,000-acre family farm and you feel not just welcome but coddled, chances are you'll be hopelessly smitten. Jimmie and Bob Booth have been offering this experience to guests for 35 years, with a prix-fixe dinner ($60, with chateaubriand, duck, lamb, or fish). It's magic. Open June-December, Tuesday-Saturday for lunch, Friday-Saturday for dinner, hayride, and cocktails at 7 P.M. Reservations a must. $$$$.

The Harvest, 37 Putnam Rd. (Rte. 44), Pomfret. 860-928-0008. Chef Peter Cooper heads up a team of cooks that will wow you every time. Peter has owned and operated excellent restaurants in the region for 10 years. He moved to this site two years ago and was quickly voted Connecticut's best new restaurant by *Connecticut Magazine*. You'll find tremendous variety here from an eclectic and international menu. Favorites include filet mignon prepared with a dry rub of 16 spices, rack of lamb, and seared salmon with Thai lemon sauce. Open year-round, closed Monday. Open Tuesday-Friday for lunch, Tuesday-Sunday for dinner, Sunday 11-2 for brunch. Reservations suggested. $$$.

Stoggy Hollow General Store & Restaurant, 492 Rte. 198, Woodstock Valley. 860-974-3814. Can't miss this hybrid general store/café/bakery where you can eat three square meals every day of the week. Choose from homemade sandwiches, soups, grilled chicken salad plate, famous french fries, and noteworthy crab cakes (recently written up in *Connecticut Magazine*). Open year-round daily, Sunday-Thursday 7 A.M.-8 P.M., Friday-Saturday 7 A.M.-9 P.M. $.

What to See

The Prudence Crandall Museum, rtes. 14 and 169, Canterbury. 860-546-9916. This first academy for black women (1833-1834) in New England was run by the remarkable Prudence Crandall. It is a National Historic Landmark, maintained by the Connecticut Historical Commission, that offers period rooms, changing exhibits, a research library, and gift shop. Open February to mid-December Wednesday-Sunday 10-4:30. $2, seniors and students $1, under 5 free.

Creamery Brook Bison, 19 Purvis Rd., Brooklyn. 860-779-0837. Austin and Debbi Tanner bought the farm in 1981 to run as a dairy. Austin's fascination with buffalo led them to raise this majestic beast. Now the buffalo herd numbers over 60. They offer a 40-minute wagon ride through the working dairy farm, sell buffalo meat, and have a gift shop. This is a great family stop. Open year-round Monday-Friday 2-6 P.M., Saturday 9-2.

Chartier Gallery, 481 Pomfret Rd. (Rtc. 169), Brooklyn. 860-779-1104. Here you will enjoy the works of noted artist and children's book illustrator Normand Chartier. The gallery is located in a 100-year-old barn in the Bush Hill Historic District, across the street from the original Israel Putnam homestead. The walls are covered with Normand's beautiful watercolors, landscapes of northeastern Connecticut and coastal Maine, painted in a semi-impressionistic style. Also on view are originals and prints of the illustrations from his children's books (50-plus titles), limited-edition prints of paintings. Open April-Christmas Thursday-Sunday noon-5, or by appointment.

Where the River Meets the Sound

The Connecticut Tidelands

SEVERAL YEARS AGO THE NATURE CONSERVANCY DE-
clared the tidelands of the Connecticut River one of the
"Last Great Places" on the globe. The locals already knew
that, of course, and are proud, if a little nervous, that their secret is out. But many of the tidelands' pleasures are under-
stated rather than obvious. People don't come here because
it's full of great events but because it's full of great places. Instead of "theme destinations," there are handsome villages
and towns. Instead of blockbuster entertainments, there are
pockets of quiet beauty.

Let's begin in Old Saybrook, where the Connecticut
spills into Long Island Sound. We'll start the morning at the

best bakery in town, Vanderbrooke Bakers and Caterers. It's tempting to eat inside amid the Vanderbrooke's yeasty aromas, but everything tastes better with sea air, so get the goodies to go and drive east down Main for a couple of miles, following the signs to Saybrook Point. Pull into the parking lot and drive right up to the edge of the land. It's one of the tidelands' most pleasing views, a lovely vista across wide waters, where the river meets the sound. Fishing boats, pleasure boats, and an occasional barge or tanker cut the horizon, as gulls wheel overhead, hoping for a piece of that good bread. The Saybrook Lighthouse, across the cove to the right, completes the nautical picture.

Midmorning may seem late to go fishing, but you're on vacation, so relax. Half the fun of fishing is talking about it. If you want to know where the blues are running or what the stripers are hitting, go to Ted's Bait and Tackle in Old Saybrook on Clark Street off Ferry Road. It's a weather-beaten, rough-hewn place frequented by commercial fishermen and weekend sportsmen. Hand-printed signs direct fishermen to herring, mummichugs, sand worms, shiners, and chum. Ted Lemelin, the owner, fishes for a living. In May, when the shad are running in the Connecticut, locals go to Ted's for their boned shad and roe, tidelands delicacies.

Time to cross the river. Take exit 70 off I-95, on the other side of the Baldwin Bridge, into Old Lyme, and turn right on Route 156 (also called Shore Road). Ferry Road comes up on the right in less than half a mile. Turn and wind down to the Department of Environmental Protection's Marine Headquarters, right on the river. But that's not the attraction tucked away here. Go for a walk on the elevated boardwalk, which traces the shoreline for half a mile. Storyboards along the way offer information about the tidelands' flora and fauna. Linger awhile and you'll see egrets, herons, ducks, and perhaps an osprey clutching a fresh-caught fish.

For more great birding, take your binoculars down to the Great Island boat launch, backtracking a bit on Route 156 to Smith Neck Road. Stand on the observation platform and

Tidelands by Water

WHAT THE LOCALS KNOW

The best way to see the tidelands is from the water. For river tours, contact the Deep River Navigation Company, which runs informative trips on the river out of Essex, Deep River, Old Saybrook, and Hartford. To explore the many marshes, coves, and small rivers, you'll need a small boat or canoe. You can rent a canoe for $35 a day at Down River Sports and Canoes on Route 154, Middlesex Square in Chester. Down River also frequently offers guided trips. Chimney Point Boat Rentals at Saybrook Marine Service in Old Saybrook rents 14-foot aluminum boats with eight-horsepower engines for $50 a day. Take binoculars, water, and sunscreen.

Deep River Navigation Company, 860-526-4954.

Down River Sports and Canoes, 860-526-1966.

Chimney Point Boat Rentals, 860-388-3614.

watch the hawks, gulls, terns, and ospreys float over the vast island marsh. More than a dozen nesting ospreys are visible from here. Twenty years ago, when the Connecticut River was a wide sewer, the ospreys had disappeared, wiped out by DDT and other pollutants. The Clean Water Act saved the river, which is now clean enough for everything except drinking. The ospreys have rebounded along with the river.

Even in the river's bad times, people still came to Sound View, the honky-tonk gene in Old Lyme's generally dignified bloodline. Take Hartford Avenue off Route 156. You'll find clam shacks, bars, and stores stuffed with beach gimcrackery. You'll also find a public beach (for a parking fee), unusual in the tidelands, where almost all the sand is private. The locals also come to Sound View for two confections sold at small storefronts — Vecchitto's Lemon Ice and the Donut Shoppe's scrumptious homemade orbs. (On weekends the early birds get the doughnuts — they're gone by 8 A.M.)

To counterbalance Sound View, drive back into Old Lyme, a quiet, shaded village. Lyme Street (the main thoroughfare) offers a gallery of American architecture — Georgian, Federal, Gothic Revival, Italianate. Many of the gracious homes, set back from the road, were built by wealthy sea captains, and the place still emanates patrician affluence.

At the turn of the century Florence Griswold began taking boarders into her mansion on Lyme Street, including some of the most famous American impressionists of the era — Childe Hassam, Willard Metcalf, Henry Ward Ranger, Will Howe Foote, William Chadwick. They came to the tidelands to paint the things that still attract visitors — the shore, the tributary streams, the marshes and coves. The Florence Griswold Museum is a small gem filled with art, including scenes painted on walls and doors by the boarding artists.

Next we're moving upriver to the village of Essex, settled in 1648. Once a thriving port of sea merchants and shipbuilders, who built the neat homes that line the narrow, shaded streets, it's now populated by yachtsmen and landlubbers attracted by Essex's marinas, Colonial charm, and the patina of wealth. Drive to the end of Main Street to the town dock and the water. It's a popular place to eat lunch and watch the river roll by; walk back up the street and pick up gourmet sandwiches at Olive Oyl's Carry Out Cuisine. But sometimes it's too hot on the dock, so drive a few blocks to the Dauntless Shipyard, past the towering dry-docked yachts and the sail makers and the yacht brokers, and eat at the Crow's Nest Gourmet Deli, on a shaded porch overlooking the river and a marina.

Don't miss the Essex Steam Train & Riverboat ride. The old locomotive chuffs for about an hour up to Deep River, too busy being a lively small town to think about yachts and patinas. You can watch the riverboats and steam train depart from the Deep River landing, where passengers board a boat for an hour-long cruise past Gillette Castle and Goodspeed Opera House.

The town of Chester, nestled prettily in a narrow notch between hills, has become chic in recent years. Like Essex, it's a pleasant place to stroll and shop. The Pattaconk 1850 Bar & Grille has been serving food and drink since 1850; sit outside or in the airy back room. For a fancy night out, try the Copper Beech Inn in Ivoryton near Essex (also a lovely place to stay) or Chester's Restaurant du Village, a small enchanting memento of Provence and a beautiful way to end a visit to the tidelands.

– *Steve Kemper*

The best way to enjoy the tidelands of Connecticut is from the water. (photo by Kindra Clineff)

Editors' Picks for the Tidelands

General Information

Connecticut Office of Tourism. Call for a free guide to the area. 800-282-6863. (ctguide.atlantic.com/vacguide)

Connecticut River Valley and Shoreline Visitors Council, 393 Main St., Middletown, CT 06457. 800-486-3346.

Where to Stay

Bee and Thistle Inn, 100 Lyme St., Old Lyme, CT 06371. 800-622-4946, 860-434-1667. This 1756 Colonial, sitting on 5½ acres overlooking the Lieutenant River, is located in the same historic district as the Florence Griswold Museum. The inn offers 11 antiques-filled guest rooms with private baths (and 1 cottage). Open year-round. $95-$155. The restaurant consistently wins kudos (voted best restaurant in the state three years in a row according to *Connecticut Magazine*'s readers' poll). Filled with plants and flowers, it features contemporary American cuisine influenced by local fish, game, and produce, all served with creativity. Open daily for breakfast; daily except Tuesday and Sunday for lunch; daily except Tuesday for dinner, Sunday 11-2 for brunch. Reservations recommended. $$$-$$$$. (www.beeandthistleinn.com)

Old Lyme Inn, 85 Lyme St., Old Lyme, CT 06371. 860-434-2600. An 1850s farmhouse located in the heart of this historic village home of American impressionism. Boasts a front porch, Victorian-style main dining area, and sitting room, grill room, and library graced with working fireplaces. All 13 guest rooms have private baths. Open year-round. Continental breakfast included. $99-$150. The inn's four-star restaurant serves classic American cuisine daily for lunch and dinner. Reservations recommended. $$$-$$$$.

Copper Beech Inn, 46 Main St., Ivoryton, CT 06442. 860-767-0330. An 1880s Victorian and carriage house on seven wooded acres with country gardens, a massive copper beech tree, and 13 guest rooms with private baths. There is a handsome Victorian-style conservatory and a gallery displaying antique Chinese porcelain. Open year-round, except first week in January. Breakfast included. $105-$175. An award-winning wine list compliments the superb country French dining at the inn's restaurant. Open Tuesday-Saturday for dinner; Sunday 1-7:30 P.M. Reservations recommended. $$$-$$$$. (www.copperbeechinn.com)

Griswold Inn, 36 Main St., Essex, CT 06426. 860-767-1776. This was the first three-story building in Connecticut and is considered the oldest continually run inn in the country. Located one block from the Connecticut River, it has 31 rooms with private baths, some with fireplaces. Breakfast included. $90-$185. Antique banners and posters, the largest private collection of Currier & Ives maritime prints in America, muskets, and nautical paintings grace the walls of the dining room. The menu highlights New England cuisine, including the best lobster roll in the area. Other favorites are kidney pie and an extensive game menu around holidaytime. Open Monday-Saturday for lunch, daily for dinner, Sunday 11-3 for brunch. Reservations recommended. $$-$$$. (www.uswelcome.com/connecti/griswol.htm)

Where to Eat

Vanderbrooke Bakers and Caterers, 65 Main St., Old Saybrook. 860-388-9700. Open Tuesday-Friday 8-5:30, Saturday 8-4; Memorial Day-Labor Day also Sunday 8-1. $.

HallMark Drive-In, Rte. 156, Old Lyme. 860-434-1998. You can find everything from burgers to clams and fresh fish and lobster rolls. Don't miss the homemade ice cream. Open March-November daily from 11 A.M. (closing time varies). $.

Luigi's, 1295 Boston Post Rd., Old Saybrook. 860-388-9190. Open in summer Tuesday-Thursday and Sunday 11-10, Friday-Saturday 11-11; in winter Tuesday-Thursday and Sunday 11-9, Friday-Saturday 11-10. $$-$$$.

Saybrook Fish House, 99 Essex Rd., Old Saybrook. 860-388-4836. Open Monday-Saturday for lunch and dinner, Sunday noon-9:30. $$-$$$.

Dock & Dine Restaurant, College St., Saybrook Point, Old Saybrook. 860-388-4665. Open daily for lunch and dinner; from Columbus Day to Easter closed Monday and Tuesday. $$-$$$.

Cuckoo's Nest, 1712 Boston Post Rd., Old Saybrook. 860-399-9060. Open daily for lunch and dinner. $$.

Olive Oyl's Carry Out Cuisine, 77 Main St., Essex. 860-767-4909. Open daily 8:30-7, except Monday. $.

Crow's Nest Gourmet Deli, 37 Pratt St., Essex. 860-767-3288. Open in summer daily 7-5, Friday-Sunday for dinner; in winter daily 7-3. $.

Pattaconk 1850 Bar & Grille, 33 Main St., Chester. 860-526-8143. Open Sunday-Thursday 11:30-9:45, Friday-Saturday 11:30-10:45. $$-$$$.

Restaurant du Village, 59 Main St., Chester. 860-526-5301. Open Tuesday-Sunday for dinner. Reservations recommended. $$$$.

What to See

Ted's Bait and Tackle, 35 Clark St., Old Saybrook. 860-388-4882. Open daily 6 A.M.-8 P.M.

Florence Griswold Museum, 96 Lyme St., Lyme. 860-434-5542. Open June-December Tuesday-Saturday 10-5. $4, seniors and students $3, under 12 and members free. (www.flogris.org)

Essex Steam Train & Riverboat, exit 3 off Rte. 9, or exit 69 off I-95, Essex. 860-767-0103. $15, children 3-11 $7.50, under 3 free.

Secrets of the Litchfield Hills

ON THE FORESTED WESTERN EDGE OF CONNECTICUT, the Litchfield Hills retain a decidedly Colonial backwoods feel. Yet perhaps because it is less than two hours from New York City, it dabbles in modernity and occasional oddity. All this creates tiny pockets of civilization hidden in the wilderness. A field of cows faces a field of sculptures. A Porsche clatters across a covered bridge, while down the road an old pickup carries the woodwind section of a New England symphony orchestra. It isn't that the culture is confused, it's just remarkably combined.

Here is a brief tour of my highlights in the area, where the majority of sights and citizens are tucked in among the hills and trees. Of the 32 towns and villages in the Litchfield area, most have fewer than 5,000 inhabitants. Of those, a wildly disproportionate number are fodder for Robin Leach. Along with executives, playwrights, musicians, authors, and heiresses, a constellation of stars have homes somewhere in these knolls: Meryl Streep, Henry Kissinger, Dustin Hoffman, and others. It is the rural nature of this northwestern corner that you don't hear much about these stars. Yet their presence has generated the growth of sophisticated shops, galleries, restaurants, and inns.

Typical of New England, this was farm country in the early 1700s and Indian country long before that. Industrialization arrived in the 1770s with the Revolutionary War, when two out of every three cannons were made from iron ore mined and smelted here. After the war, many Litchfield families prospered in commerce and the China Trade. By the end of the 19th century, as the industrial revolution evolved, the shift to water power on the Connecticut River left Litchfield hill towns unspoiled. The resulting calm attracted a new clientele, the rich and powerful who came to relax and a legion of artists who came to create. Eventually tourists came to see what all these other people were up to.

On the eastern side of the county, the area is at once more industrial and more remote. For instance, a local claimed there were 63 homes in the village of Riverton. Looking around, I concluded that he must have counted beaver lodges. The Hitchcock Chair Company, one of the best-known names in Early American furniture, survives here. The factory (showroom) and adjacent store sit on the banks of the Farmington River, where Lambert Hitchcock began the business in 1818. It is interesting to note that by then the Old Riverton Inn had been in operation for 22 years, taking in passengers from the Hartford-Albany stagecoach. Today the inn, on the National Register of Historic Places, still welcomes leaf peepers, trout fishermen, and other visitors.

Torrington, Litchfield County's largest city (with 33,000 residents), is a place that gets bad press or no press.

Window-Box Wars

The shopkeepers of Litchfield and New Preston are at war over window boxes. This fierce horticultural rivalry gets worse every year, and locals and visitors love every minute of it. If you stroll downtown Litchfield early in the morning, you are likely to see half a dozen shopkeepers grooming their window boxes. In nearby New Preston shopkeepers retaliate by arming themselves with secret fertilizing formulas and deadheading devices. As far as anyone can figure, the window-box wars began in New Preston about ten years ago when a certain antiques dealer achieved fame in *The New Yorker* for his window boxes. Not to be outdone, Litchfield's West Street Grill put $50 rosemary plants in theirs. It didn't take long before others were inspired — daisies, cosmos, geraniums, cascading petunias, white cleome, nasturtiums, dwarf varieties, and other rarities make for masterpieces. A few years ago one merchant planted so early that he had to build a burlap tent to protect the plants at night. Don't think that a couple of strolls will satisfy. Most merchants put out new versions in spring, summer, and fall.

– Tovah Martin

Factories and stores have closed and people have moved on, but the city is enjoying a mini renaissance of sorts. And some businesses endure — the Yankee Pedlar Inn — an 1891 hotel, where the rates are reasonable and the hotel bar is friendly. You can eat at the inn or just around the corner, and worth a trip to Torrington in itself is the Venetian Restaurant. Here I am always served healthy portions of exceptional Italian food, surrounded by beautifully painted murals and a charming pressed-tin ceiling.

Ten miles southwest of Torrington, back in the country, is another of my Litchfield favorites — the rural farming town of Morris. Lined with Colonial houses, old barns, and stone walls, Route 109 could be in central Pennsylvania — except for that pasture with the naked female in it.

Lorenz (Larry) LiVolsi is the cause of this interest. In the fields on his farm are an elephant, a multipiece rusting metal sculpture, a female mannequin suspended in midair by an iron rod in a boulder, and about two dozen or so other sculptures. Two of Larry's pieces are cared for by the Smithsonian Institution's "Save Outdoor Sculpture" in public places program. LiVolsi is one of the region's myriad artists, and these works are his calling cards. His work, however, is not the only attraction. Every year Larry and his wife, Stephanie, lead a unique (they call it "underground") Fourth of July parade from Lorenz Studios to the post office about a mile down the road. The procession features more than 300 marchers — many writers and artists from New York mixed in with the locals — and "floats," actually sculptures by LiVolsi and friends.

These eerie floating mannequins are the work of sculptor Larry LiVolsi of Lorenz Studios. *(photo courtesy Larry LiVolsi, Lorenz Studios)*

Another favorite is the town of Woodbury, where along Route 6 I can't say "toby jugs" before passing another antiques shop. Here I give myself a whole day (but it could take a week) for browsing jewelry, collectibles, decorative arts, curios, and three centuries of furnishings.

Litchfield is a postcard town, another quintessential New England village with its green, church, and enormous, impeccably cared for old houses. If Litchfield's much-photographed Congregational church hadn't already put this town on the map, the gourmet offerings of the popular West Street Grill would have.

And now the town of Kent. It is certainly not unusual in America for a town of 3,000 to have an art gallery. But tiny Kent has ten art galleries (a little migration from SoHo has transplanted here). This village is the Litchfield Hills in miniature, from the covered Bull's Bridge on the south end to the art and antiques downtown, to Kent Falls in the north. All around are high ridges that practically get down on their knolls and beg to be photographed when the foliage fires up around Columbus Day. Kent and the towns to its north constitute Connecticut's "mountain region," where verdant ridges pierce the skies and radio reception staggers and dies.

From Bear Mountain in Salisbury, at 2,316 feet, you can see three states — scenery is what this corner of the northwest corner is all about. But just when I think this part of the state holds some truly untamed wilderness, both in its woods and its people, the signs of polite civilization reappear. On a bulletin board outside the West Cornwall post office I see hand-printed index cards and stylized flyers: bridge partners wanted, nanny needed, wine tasting Saturday, antique book sale today. Another sign promotes a woodwind concert in the forest, not an unusual event for the Litchfield Hills, where I am beginning to get used to finding Tchaikovsky in my tree house.

– Andrew Marlatt

Editors' Picks for the Litchfield Hills

General Information

Litchfield Hills Travel Council, P.O. Box 968, Litchfield, CT 06759. 860-567-4506. Visitor information booth, located on the green in Litchfield, open mid-June to October. (www.litchfieldhills.com)

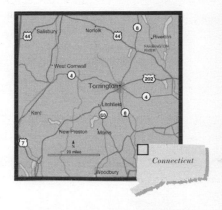

Where to Stay

Old Riverton Inn, Rte. 20, Box 6, Riverton, CT 06065. 800-378-1796, 860-379-8678. Two hundred years of hospitality for the hungry, thirsty, and sleepy. There are 12 guest rooms, all with private baths. Open year-round. Full breakfast included. $85-$180. The restaurant serves hearty, traditional fare, including steaks, seafood, and pasta. Open year-round Wednesday-Saturday for lunch and dinner, Sunday noon-8. $$-$$$. (www.newenglandinns.com/inns/riverton/index.html)

Yankee Pedlar Inn, 93 Main St., Torrington, CT 06790. 800-777-1891, 860-489-9226. A charming 60-room full-service hotel set in the historic downtown area. Big fireplace in lobby with roaring fire all winter long, gift shop, and visitor information on premises. Open year-round. Continental buffet breakfast included. $69-$139. Conley's Pub & Restaurant offers wonderful American food; specialty is rack of lamb. Restaurant open Monday-Saturday for lunch and dinner. $-$$$. (www.pedlarinn.com)

Mayflower Inn, Rte. 47 (just off the village green), Wood-bury Rd., Washington, CT 06793. 860-868-9466. This pres-tigious country-house hotel was built in 1894 and offers 25 antiques-appointed guest rooms and suites. Set on 30 very private acres with award-winning restaurant, dining rooms, fitness club, tennis court, outdoor heated pool, and walking trails. Open year-round. $270-$450, suites $450-$670. The Mayflower's restaurant serves New American cuisine with an Asian influence. Open for lunch and dinner. $$-$$$$. (www.integra.fr/relaischateaux/mayflower)

Manor House, 69 Maple Ave., Norfolk, CT 06058. 860-542-5690. An 1898 English Tudor on 5½ acres, with Vic-torian architecture, six-foot living-room fireplace, and Tiffany windows. All eight rooms have private baths, some with fireplaces, Jacuzzi, and private balconies. Visitors enjoy hiking, biking, swimming, perennial gardens, and in the win-ter, cross-country skiing and horse-drawn sleigh rides. Open year-round. Breakfast included. $110-$195.

Chaucer House, 88 N. Main St. (Rte. 7), Kent, CT 06757. 860-927-4858. This comfortable Colonial with three guest rooms, all with private baths, is conveniently located in town, where you can park your car (once) and walk to gal-leries, restaurants, and shops. Open year-round. Full break-fast included. $70-$90.

Where to Eat

Venetian Restaurant, 52 East Main St., Torrington. 860-489-8592. People drive miles for their superb, authentic Ital-ian cuisine. Specialties include savory grilled lamb chops, veal, osso buco, and tiramisu. Voted the best Italian restau-rant in the county for 10 years in a row by *Connecticut Maga-zine*. Large murals grace the walls. Open every day except Tuesday for lunch and dinner. $-$$$.

West Street Grill, 43 West St. (on the green), Litchfield. 860-567-3885. According to many visitors and national food critics, this is one of the best restaurants in the state and has been named one of America's top restaurants by *Condé Nast Traveler.* It specializes in a natural approach, cooking with fresh herbs and local, organic ingredients. Open daily for lunch and dinner. $-$$$.

Spinell's Litchfield Food Company, 39 West St. (on the green), Litchfield. 860-567-3113. A not-to-miss café, bakery, gourmet store, and catering business. Hearty homemade soups, salads, entrées, sandwiches, breads, and pastries. Dine in the café or take out to a perfect picnic spot. Open daily 8-6, except Wednesday. $.

Bulls Bridge Inn, 333 Kent Rd., Kent. 860-927-1000. Located across the street from the historic covered bridge. A cozy tavern that features steaks, chicken, fresh grilled seafood, salad bar, and tap room with copper-topped bar. Open year-round for dinner. $$.

Fife 'n' Drum Restaurant and Inn, 53 N. Main St. (Rte. 7), Kent. 860-927-3509. Family owned and operated since 1972, the Fife features tableside service, and specialties include Caesar salad, rack of lamb, *filet au poivre*, and a list of 500 wines. Open every day except Tuesday for lunch and dinner; Sunday 11:30-9 (brunch 11:30-3, $16.95 per person). $-$$$.

Le Bon Coin, 223 Litchfield Turnpike (Rte. 202), New Preston. 860-868-7763. Voted best Litchfield County French restaurant by *Connecticut Magazine* readers' poll for five years in a row. Classic French cuisine in an intimate, cozy atmosphere with an extensive wine list. Le Bon Coin has been owned and operated by chef William Janega since 1983. Open Thursday-Saturday for lunch and dinner; Sunday 5-9 P.M.; open during foliage season Sunday 1-9 P.M. $-$$$.

What to See

Lorenz Studios, Rte. 109, Lakeside (a hamlet of Morris). 860-567-4280. Visit the studio of glassblower and sculptor Larry LiVolsi. Here you can roam the fantastic outdoor sculpture garden, watch Larry at work in his studio, and stop in at the gallery that displays and sells blown glass, sculpture, unique furnishings, and paintings by Stephanie Kafka. Open year-round Tuesday-Sunday 10-5 (or by appointment).

Antiques, nearly every town in Litchfield County has at least one antiques shop, and many towns have several. You'll find the largest concentration in Woodbury, followed by the towns of New Preston and Litchfield. For a complete listing of shops send for the brochure: *The Litchfield Hills UNWIND Connecticut* from the Litchfield Hills Travel Council.

Glebe House Museum and Gertrude Jekyll Garden, Hollow Rd. (off Rte. 6), Woodbury. 203-263-2855. Architecturally interesting, this 1770s minister's farmhouse, or glebe, was where the first American bishop of the Episcopal church was elected in 1750. The house has fine period furnishings, original paneling, gift shop, and the only garden in the United States designed by Gertrude Jekyll. Open April-November Wednesday-Sunday 1-4 P.M. $5, children 6-12 $2.

Rhode Island

Waterplace Park, Providence (photo by Jim McElholm, courtesy Providence Convention and Visitors Bureau)

The Exotic Flavors of Providence

A New World of Eating in This City of Immigrants

~

THE MAN BEHIND THE COUNTER IS WAITING FOR ME to make up my mind. Yucca or cassava? I motion: a little of each. My plate is already groaning — a Jackson Pollock of rice, fried plantains, crackle-skinned suckling pig, goat stew, and onion gravy.

It's a gray afternoon in Providence and it's late for lunch. But no matter, Carolina is brimming with "la vida." Almost everyone at this Dominican ladle house is Latino and male. Some are off to factory jobs, others are headed home with leaky Styrofoam boxes. Of the several places on upper

Broad, Carolina is said to be the best, though La Gran Parada across the street gets raves for its tripe. These cheap cafeterias are named for the hearty stews they serve ladled over rice. I've been to Providence more times than I can count, but this is my first ladle house.

The plan was quite simple: I was going to eat my way through town with help from Sean and Anne, my foodie brother-in-law and his wife, who live in nearby Barrington, and from Barbara Kuck, curator of the treasure-laden Culinary Archives & Museum at Johnson & Wales University. Barbara really knows her way around the unsung ethnic markets, bakeries, delis, restaurants, and ladle houses of Providence. Vietnamese, Salvadoran, Russian, Portuguese, Italian — all of it is here within a 15-minute drive from downtown. What I couldn't scarf down in a ladylike fashion, I'd sock away in the trunk. A Honda makes a very handy portable Frigidaire.

Barbara and I began our day of gluttony at Portuguese American Market. I marveled over the breads — a dense, sour cornmeal loaf, rough Portuguese rolls, and *palitos de cintra*, sweet lemony dunkers for coffee, while Barbara, a denizen of this area, got us a mess of her favorite coconut and citrus tartlets.

Five minutes later we were in downtown Cranston at Near East Market. It was like coming home. Here was food I grew up with as a pudgy Armenian child: creamy Bulgarian feta, ground lamb pizzas, known as *lahmejun*, and enormous brown-paper-wrapped wheels of cracker bread.

Heading back north to Elmwood and South Providence, we ducked into La Famosa on Broad Street for sweets. Broad Street is the ethnic soul of the city: Latin on one end, Asian on the other, and a bit scrappy all the way down the line. Half the fun at La Famosa is filling a paper bag penny-candy-style, so we indulged.

After we whizzed back down Broad, in the heart of Little Asia was the object of my desire: the closet-size Wing Kee, with five ducks glazed a rich mahogany in the window and a small shrine to Buddha with incense and offerings on the lone shelf inside. "Whole or half?" asked the slight Simon Chan. Wielding the cleaver with amazing strength, he made fast work of slicing and had wrapped the succulent pieces in white paper in no time. No surprise — Simon and his wife, Sandy, have been barbecuing ducks for 17 years.

The next day we set out en famille along Atwells Avenue on Federal Hill, Providence's Little Italy. Much of the city's considerable Italian population was there picking up provisions for a big Sunday lunch. We did our part, nibbling all the way. At Venda Ravioli, one of the newer shops on De Pasquale Avenue — check out the painting of the Creation from the Sistine chapel ceiling above the outdoor café — we bought homemade asparagus-filled ravioli, smelly Abruzzese (highly touted by the woman next to me who seemed to know her sausages), and a bag of fresh capers, cured in salt, not brine. Once you've thrown these plump lovelies into puttanesca sauce (rinse them first), there's no going back.

At the other end of the spectrum and the other end of the square, Antonelli's Poultry Co. provides an authentic old-time experience, which means it's not for the faint-hearted. The back room smells like a henhouse and looks like one, too, with cages of live geese, ducks, rabbits, and

Juana Brito owns La Famosa on Broad Street, where you can sample treats such as toasted coconut macaroons and guava squares. (photo by Kindra Clineff)

chickens that the butcher will slaughter to order right before your eyes. Out front, the squeamish can buy chicken, fresh chicken and duck eggs, and Latin American and African groceries like Nigerian yam flour for fritters.

Back on Atwells a block or so up, Carmina Conti, an employee of Providence Cheese Gourmet Foods, was rolling out sheets of red-pepper pasta for ravioli. Conti, who was born in Rome, is a relative newcomer. She started cooking in the early 1980s at the shop that Frank Basso Wheatley established in 1912. Later, Wheatley's daughter Ginny took over, and now her son Wayne owns it with his wife, Patrizia, who also happens to be Conti's daughter. One of the best things about the place is that you can mix and match pastas and fillings to order. We went for red pepper stuffed with spinach ricotta and watched the ravioli wheel do its thing. Barely big enough to move around in, Providence Cheese is a visual feast: mascarpone and Gorgonzola torta in the glass case, prosciuttos and provolones hooked on the ceiling, homemade pepperoncini stuffed with pecorino and prosciutto in jars, everything looking like an Italian grandma made it. Frank Wheatley was an early health-food convert, and to this day, pastas and baked goods are made with whole wheat flour, desserts sweetened with dried and fresh fruits.

Backtracking, we made our way to Tony's Colonial Food Store, a tour de force of marketing and genuine quality. Tony's is the only shop on Federal Hill to have a flashy billboard at Providence's airport. The shelves are stocked to the gills with imported jams, pastas, sauces, vinegars, oils, cookbooks, and Italian ceramics and glass. Dozens of imported hams, salamis, mortadellas, and cheeses swing from the rafters.

After such excess, Palmieri's Bakery a few blocks away is pleasantly austere. This plain old-style bakery has been making fine-textured Italian loaves, wine and pepper biscuits, spinach pies, and not much else in its large brick ovens since the turn of the century. Right now, the third generation is in charge, but Palmieri's still reminds me of a shop you'd see in a small Tuscan town.

There was one last stop: the Russian Market all the way out on Hope Street, which turns into East Avenue in Pawtucket. Here amid bags of Ukrainian sour rye, platters of smoked herring, German wursts, Polish cheeses, and jars of sour cherries, I had my last lunch, sitting at the single table. The motherly Tatyana Nazo brought over dishes of salad russe (a sort of beet, potato, onion salad) and pillowy blintzes crammed not with cheese but with soul-satisfying globs of chopped liver.

Time to leave. The trunk was loaded, my husband waiting, much of my mission accomplished. I hadn't made it to every last place on my dance card, but that was a good reason to come back. And now I had another: chopped-liver blintzes.

– Cynthia Hacinli

Editors' Picks for Providence

General Information

Providence Warwick Convention & Visitors' Bureau, 1 American Express Way, Waterplace Park (mailing address: 1 West Exchange St.), Providence, RI 02903. 800-233-1636 (out-of-state only), 401-274-1636; in-state Visitor Information Center, 401-751-1177. (www.providencecvb.com)

Where to Stay

Westin Hotel Providence, 1 West Exchange St., Providence, RI 02903. 401-598-8000. One of the finest works of contemporary architecture around. Centrally located with 364 rooms and suites. The only AAA four-diamond property in the state. $149-$260. (Weekend packages also available.) Award-winning restaurant Agora is open Monday-Thursday 5:30-9:30 P.M., Friday-Saturday 5:30-10 P.M. $$$-$$$$. (www.swift-tourism.com/westin/providence.htm)

Old Court Bed & Breakfast, 144 Benefit St., Providence, RI 02903. 401-751-2002. This 1863 Italianate mansion is right on Benefit Street, a quiet neighborhood, and near most of what you will want to see. The 11 antiques-furnished rooms have a variety of styles, and all have private baths. Open year-round. Breakfast included. $90-$140. (www.oldcourt.com)

The Providence Biltmore, Kennedy Plaza, 11 Dorrance St., Providence, RI 02903. 800-294-7709 (reservations only), 401-421-0700. Built in 1922, this classic hotel has just been brought back to life in a dazzling restoration. Crystal, gilding, and marble give the public areas elegance, and the 244 large, well-appointed rooms have all the amenities. $120-$210. Special packages available. (www.grandheritage.com)

State House Inn, 43 Jewett St., Providence, RI 02908. 401-351-6111. An 1889 neo-Colonial on a quarter acre located in a historic neighborhood; 15-minute walk to downtown Providence and Waterplace Park. The inn has 10 rooms with private baths and two working fireplaces. Open year-round. Breakfast included. $99-$129.

Where to Eat

Carolina, 864 Broad St., Providence. 401-941-1333. Open daily 8 A.M.-10 P.M.

La Gran Parada, 937 Broad St., Providence. 401-941-4610. Open 10 A.M.-8 P.M.

Portuguese American Market, 896 Allens Ave., Providence. 401-941-4480. Open daily 8-8.

Near East Market, 602 Reservoir Ave., Cranston. 401-941-9763. Open Monday-Saturday 9 A.M.-6 P.M., Sunday 9-2.

La Famosa, 1035 Broad St., Providence. 401-941-4550. Open daily 8 A.M.-10 P.M.

Sanchez Market, 676 Broad St., Providence. 401-831-5470. Open daily 8 A.M.-10 P.M.

Aspara, 716 Public St., Providence. 401-785-1490. Open Sunday-Thursday 10 A.M.-9:30 P.M., Friday and Saturday 10-10.

Wing Kee, 312 Broad St., Providence. 401-751-8688. Open Monday-Friday 10:30-6.

Venda Ravioli, 265 Atwells Ave., Providence. 401-421-9105. Open Monday 9-6, Tuesday-Saturday 8:30-6, Sunday 8:30-2.

Antonelli's Poultry Co., 62 De Pasquale Ave., Providence. 401-421-8739. Open Tuesday-Saturday 8-5.

Providence Cheese Gourmet Foods, 178 Atwells Ave., Providence. 401-421-5653. Open Monday-Friday 9-6, Saturday 9-5 during summer; Monday-Friday 9-6, Saturday 9-5, Sunday 10-2 the rest of the year.

Tony's Colonial Food Store, 311 Atwells Ave., Providence. 401-621-8675. Open Monday-Saturday 8:30-6, Sunday 8:30-4.

Palmieri's Bakery, 147 Ridge St., Providence. 401-831-9145. Open Tuesday-Friday 6:30-5:30, Saturday 6:30-4:30, Sunday 6:30-12:30, closed Mondays.

Sanchez Tortilleria, 802 Atwells Ave., Providence. 401-331-6469. Open Monday-Saturday 8 A.M.-9 P.M., Sunday 8-5.

Russian Market, 727 East Ave., Pawtucket. 401-723-9870. Open Monday-Saturday 9-8, Sunday 10-4.

What to See

Culinary Archives & Museum at Johnson & Wales University, 315 Harborside Blvd., Providence, RI 02905. 401-598-2805. Open Monday-Friday 9-5, Saturday 10-5, closed major holidays. $5, seniors $4, college students with ID $2, children 5-18 $1. Group tours available with special rates. (No photographs permitted.) There are plans to move to a new building, so be sure to call ahead. (www.culinary.org)

Antiques Hunting in East Bay

Treasures Just East of Providence

BARRINGTON, WARREN, AND BRISTOL, ALL LOCATED on Route 114 between Providence and Newport, make up East Bay. Barrington is largely a bedroom community for Providence; Warren is authentic New England at its best; and Bristol is a historic seaport with all the amenities of a tourist town. Though these Bristol County towns share Narragansett Bay, miles of salt marshes dotted with shorebirds, a 14-mile scenic bike path, and stunning architecture, I haven't come for these outdoor pleasures. I have come here because of antiques.

Of East Bay's three towns, Warren and Bristol offer

the best destinations for antiquing. You'll stroll among historic buildings, have a snack in a local café, and take in views of sailboats along the waterfronts. The pace is more conducive to browsing than the usual hopping in and out of the car in antiques alleys. Take time to talk to the dealers. Antiques shops are characterized by their owners. These are people who appreciate tradition and the musty smell of a warm attic. Antiques dealers are lovers of surprise, escorts on a treasure hunt. They know about hope and disappointment. They also know about loving and losing. All the dealers I met could recall their first antique, and none still owned it. Consider them foster parents, giving a cherished object a temporary home until someone comes along who shares their appreciation.

Warren

It all started in Warren with Gil Warren, who for 33 years has been the heart of antiques in East Bay. On a sunny day you'll find him sitting in front of the Square Peg on the corner of Water and Miller streets. Gil's laugh is infectious, his manner unassuming, and his shop jam-packed with a month's worth to see.

Inside, I ask about his favorites, and he says with a grin, "The last 20 things I bought." He points to a cast-iron rabbit garden ornament, faded off-white with pink eyes, "probably painted five times." There is another rabbit, about eight inches tall, primitively carved of wood, in a case next to a papier-mâché rabbit. Gil really doesn't have a thing about rabbits; he can't afford to have a "thing" about any one piece. "I'd go broke if I kept all the things I like," he explains. He has artifacts from the Fall River steamboat line, thousands of antique buttons ranging in price from 5¢ to $30, fountain pens, watches, lead soldiers, Gorham silver, and literally hundreds of other things. He is a generalist: "You'll find something here you want — and maybe even something you need."

Warren's Architectural Gem

WHAT THE LOCALS KNOW

Gary Budlong, manager of the Square Peg, is a town expert on Warren's history and architecture. Anybody who chats with him has the good fortune of finding a spontaneous tour guide. "Warren has an excellent representation of architecture from 1680 on," he says, and advises, "Don't miss the Methodist church, an 1844 Greek Revival, Christopher Wren-type building, and the George Hail Library, a gem of a Victorian — looks as if Richardson's Trinity Church [in Boston] had a puppy." He encourages visitors to the shop to walk around the corner and see the town's first fire engine, Little Hero, dating from 1802 and housed in the Fire Museum on Baker Street. And he is right about not missing another little gem in Warren, the Touisset Marsh, a 67-acre Audubon preserve, where I saw a blue heron, a snowy egret, and cormorants.

Sandra Nathanson opened the Lady Next Door right around the corner on Water Street 12 years ago. She named her shop after Gil's constant recommendation to his customers to "see the lady next door." Here female inventory reigns — vintage clothes of sumptuous velvet, satin, and silk; shoes, handbags, and stacks of textiles and linens; glassware, toys, dolls, and jewelry.

Sandra is a set decorator who has worked on numerous historic dramas, including *The Scarlet Letter* for WGBH in Boston. "My interest in antiques came out of costume research," she explains, "and I started collecting props." As she walks around the crowded shop, Sandra points out an m.i.b. (mint in box) Chein drummer. "I just love this one," she says, as she looks over a shelf packed with tin windup toys and little stuffed animals with bald spots and matted fur. "The wonderful thing about antiques is that in just one old object I am told a story," she says. "It is the small everyday things that capture entire lives."

Gil meets me as I walk out of Sandra's shop. He holds a brilliant blue creamer with a Shirley Temple transfer image on the front. He picked it up at an auction in Newport the night before and wants to see what Sandra thinks of it. "The color is too blue," she quickly observes, "and the dots on the transfer are too big." Gil replies, "I thought it was new, too, but the woman I bought it from said she got it from her grandmother." He shrugs. "I'm always learning," he says.

On the corner of Miller and Main streets Jane Ryan runs the Warren Antique Center Inc., a group shop representing more than 100 dealers. Booths and cases fill the 1920s movie theater, renovated so all three floors and balcony are exposed. Here there is everything from big pieces (downstairs) to jewelry, maps, pottery, tools, and collectibles, most of it displayed behind glass. At the Warren Antique Center be sure to pick up a comprehensive guide that Albert has assembled; it contains information about local shops and restaurants.

There are at least a dozen more antiques shops in Warren, including one of the best card and comics stores in New England, plus Jamiel's (a huge family shoe store), the Samsonite factory outlet, and Warren Chair Works.

Bristol

In Bristol I stopped first at Dantiques, run for 20 years by Christine and Dan Manchester. The Manchesters have demonstrated longevity in a fickle business by offering a little bit of everything. "We turn over at least half our merchandise each month," says Dan, who buys primarily through private homes and estate sales. "Antiques just go with Bristol," says Dan. "We are a historic area. Our families have lived in the same houses for generations. Now these homes are beginning to change hands, and their furnishings are turning up in our shops."

I found James Dumas behind the counter of Jesse James Antiques, caning the seat of a circa 1860 grain-painted Empire chair. His head was bowed in concentration. At any given time there might be as many as 25 chairs in the back room of Jesse James awaiting new life, but chairs are only a small part of the inventory. Partner Jesse Miranda spoke as James kept working, "We have china, linens, jewelry, silver, and furniture," pointing to a big Early Victorian cupboard made of golden-colored ash. Inside, flowered English china plates sat in a row.

Alfred Brazil, another Bristol native, has been selling antiques for 25 years. His main shop, Alfred's, is housed in a neatly restored yellow clapboard building on Hope Street. Inside, mahogany furniture (a specialty), cut glass, silver, Limoges, collectibles, and gifts (new) pack three big rooms. It is unusual for an antiques shop to offer new items, but many of the gifts Alfred sells are reproduction ornaments or exclusives and are related to Christmas. "I like Christmas," Alfred says with understatement. "Every day is like Christmas here — for surprise," he smiles, "is the best part of this business."

– Polly Bannister

Gil Warren put the town of Warren on the map as an antiques mecca when he opened his shop, the Square Peg, 35 years ago.
(photo by Kindra Clineff)

Editors' Picks for East Bay

General Information

East Bay Chamber of Commerce, 654 Metacom Ave., Suite 2, Warren, RI 02885-2316. 888-278-9948, 401-245-0750. (www.eastbaychamber.org)

Where to Stay

Nathaniel Porter Inn, 125 Water St., Warren, RI 02885. 401-245-6622. Considered one of the state's best-preserved Colonial homes, this inn has three rooms — each with private bath — and a very good restaurant. Open year-round. Breakfast included. $80. Special package for two (includes continental breakfast and two dinner entrées) $99.

Candlewick Inn, 775 Main St., Warren, RI 02885. 401-247-2425. There are three rooms available in this charming turn-of-the-century Sears-kit home, one private bath, one shared. Open year-round. Full gourmet breakfast included. $75-$115.

The Parker Borden House, 736 Hope St., Bristol, RI 02809. 401-253-2084. A recently restored circa 1798 Federal with three rooms, one with private bath. Has a water view and is located across from East Bay Bike Path. Open year-round. Breakfast included. $70-$85 shared bath, $95 private bath.

The Rockwell House Inn, 610 Hope St., Bristol, RI 02809. 800-815-0040, 401-253-0040. This circa 1809 Federal Victorian is located in the heart of Bristol, with four rooms, all with private baths. Some have fireplaces, and the innkeepers provide bathrobes and hair dryers, serve sherry, and offer a gourmet breakfast. You'll find the largest and oldest tulip poplar tree in the state right in the backyard here. Open year-round. Breakfast included. $85-$135.

Bradford-Dimond-Norris House, 474 Hope St., Bristol, RI 02809. 888-329-6338, 401-253-6338. This circa 1792 building is one of Bristol's best-known landmarks, called the "Wedding Cake House." It has four guest rooms, all with private baths and central air-conditioning. Open year-round. Breakfast included. $70-$100. (www.edgenet.net/bdnhouse)

Where to Eat

Redlefsen's Rotisserie and Grill, 444 Thames St., Bristol. 401-254-1188. This restaurant is highly recommended by locals and visitors alike, who enjoy the European bistro atmosphere. Its Wiener schnitzel has been called the best in New England. Open Tuesday-Saturday for lunch, Tuesday-Sunday 5-9:30 P.M. for dinner. $$-$$$.

Quito's Restaurant, 411 Thames St., Bristol. 401-253-4500. Don't be misled by plastic chairs and paper plates. The seafood is so fresh that you can watch it being unloaded from Quito's boat right on Bristol Harbor; it is also a wholesale fish market. Open May-September Sunday, Monday, Wednesday-Saturday for lunch and dinner; October-April Thursday-Sunday for lunch and dinner. $-$$.

Golden Goose Deli, 365 Hope St., Bristol. 401-253-1414. For more than 10 years this place has been voted as having the best deli sandwich in the East Bay. We recommend Pilgrim's Pride, an oven-roasted turkey sandwich with home-made stuffing and cranberry sauce. Open daily 9-9; in winter 9-8; closed only on major holidays. $.

Where to Shop

It is always a good idea to call ahead — antiques shopkeepers often keep "flexible" hours, and we wouldn't want you to be disappointed.

In Warren

The Square Peg, 51 Miller St. (No phone.) Open most days noon-5.

The Lady Next Door, 196 Water St. 401-831-7338. Open Thursday-Saturday 1-5 P.M.

Water Street Antiques, 147-149 Water St. 401-245-6440. Open most days 10-6.

Warren Antique Center, 5 Miller St. 401-245-5461. Free entertainment Friday nights. Open Saturday-Thursday 10-5; Friday 10-9; closed major holidays.

Marie King Antiques and Horsefeathers, 382 Main St. 401-245-1020, 401-245-5530. Both shops open Tuesday-Saturday 10-5, Sunday noon-5; in winter Tuesday-Sunday noon-5.

Two Guys Sports Cards & Comics, 36 Market St. 401-247-2780. Open Monday-Friday noon-6, Saturday 11-5, Sunday noon-4.

Yankee Consignments, 18 Child St. or 21 Market St. (two entrances). 401-245-6569. Used furniture, but some antiques in the 200-plus-piece inventory; great prices. Open Monday-Saturday 10-5, Sunday noon-5. Another shop with a similar kind of inventory now exists in the basement of this same store and is aptly named Tony's Cellar.

In Bristol

Dantiques, 676 Hope St. 401-253-1122. Open Tuesday-Saturday 10-4.

Jesse James Antiques, 44 State St. 401-253-2240. Open Monday-Saturday 10-5, Sunday noon-5.

Alfred's, 401-327-331 Hope St. 401-253-3465. Open Monday-Saturday 10-5, Sunday noon-5.

Sweetbrier, 317 Hope St. 401-253-1904. Summer hours: Monday by chance; Tuesday, Wednesday, and Saturday 11-5; Thursday and Friday 11-8; Sunday noon-5. Winter hours: Monday by chance; Tuesday, Wednesday, Thursday, and Saturday 11-5:30; Friday 11-8; Sunday noon-5.

Stickney & Stickney, 295 Hope St. 401-254-0179. Open Tuesday-Saturday 11-5, Sunday noon-5.

Center Chimney Antiques, 39 State St. 401-253-8010. Fine antiques and collectibles sold by John and Leonora White. Open Monday-Friday 1-5:30 P.M., Saturday noon-5.

Robin Jenkins Antiques, 278 Hope St. 401-254-8958. Specializes in garden and architectural pieces and primitives. Open Tuesday-Saturday 11-5:30, Sunday noon-5; open Monday and evenings by chance or appointment.

The Most Beautiful Port

Newport Refuses to Live in the Past

NEARLY EVERY TIME I DRIVE ACROSS THE PELL BRIDGE to Newport, I think of a long-ago boss of mine, a man whose first view of Newport was the same one I see from the crest of the bridge. He was driving from New Haven, Connecticut, to a job interview in Newport, and as he took in the vision ahead of him, he decided then and there that he would live in Newport whether he got the job or not.

I believe it: That same scene — which I have seen hundreds, probably thousands of times — still makes me want to check to be sure my mouth isn't hanging open. Newport from that vantage point looks like a 19th-century painting: Narragansett Bay is dotted with islands and speckled with sailboats; the city, sweeping uphill from the busy harbor, is surprisingly dense with trees; and smack in the middle, the 150-foot spire of the 1726 Trinity Church rises among scores of Colonial houses.

Of course Newport is an active participant in the 20th century. Too active, some might say, what with the proliferation of T-shirt shops up and down Thames Street, where, just a few decades ago, the most popular businesses catered to sailors and fishermen looking for a safe port and a stiff drink. Still, Newport radiates the spirit that has drawn people to the city for almost four centuries.

Newport has had more than one set of glory days. First there was the Colonial era, when the city was an important seaport, a point in the triangle trade, a home to many wealthy merchants, and a haven for those looking for religious freedom. Then there was the famous Gilded Age, when Astors and Vanderbilts ruled the social scene from their splashy summer "cottages" on Bellevue Avenue, each more ostentatious than the last in the ultimate display of keeping up with the Joneses. (Some say that phrase comes from here: The first of these palaces, the 1839 Kingscote, was owned by a man named George Noble Jones.) In this century, Newport has gained fame as a sailing capital, though I fear that the city's true claim to that title ended with the loss of the America's Cup in 1983.

Yet this is hardly a dusty attic of history. Newport's best quality may be its cheerful refusal to let all that glory lie in the past. In the city's eyes, it still is a Colonial power, a playground for the wealthy, a sporting town of gentleman sailors. And it's so easy for a visitor to be charmed into agreeing. This is a great city for walking, and when you've got the cobblestones of Thames Street under your feet, you can almost hear the past clip-clop of horses.

The Point Section is lined with houses in a wealth of architectural styles, from tiny Colonials that sag and bulge to tall Victorians with generous gingerbread trim and fresh paint. Gardens are a specialty in this neighborhood. Poke your nose over fences and down driveways and discover lovely surprises. You can even take a peek inside: Visit the Hunter House, a magnificent Colonial built in 1748 that often gets overlooked in favor of the Bellevue Avenue mansions. The large rooms hold more Newport-made 18th-century Townsend-Goddard furniture than you'll see anywhere else, and one room displays the first commissioned painting by Gilbert Stuart, the Rhode Island artist best known for the portrait of George Washington on the $1 bill.

If you're wandering the Point Section at dinnertime, look for the Rhumb Line. Tourists don't usually find this restaurant because it's just off the beaten track, and that means you've got a shot at being seated without a reservation. It's cozy and relaxed, serving continental and American fare, including a good selection of seafood dishes.

Walk down Thames Street; everybody does. But keep walking: Once you get eight or ten blocks beyond Memorial

Marble House, built for William K. Vanderbilt in the late 1890s, still has its original furnishings. (photo by John Corbett, courtesy Preservation Society of Newport County)

Touro Synagogue is well-known for being the oldest synagogue in North America, and its interior is one of the finest works of Colonial restoration in New England. (photo by John T. Hopf, courtesy Society of Friends of Touro Synagogue)

Boulevard — don't worry, they're short blocks — the T-shirt and ice-cream shops give way to antiques, vintage clothing, and fine arts and crafts. Two favorite stops: The Armchair Sailor bookstore (543 Thames St.) has a good selection of books with a Newport theme, and Aardvark Antiques (475 Thames St.) has an enormous outdoor display of garden statuary.

From Thames, it's only two blocks east to Bellevue Avenue and the opulent mansions. The Breakers and Marble House, built in the 1890s for Vanderbilt brothers Cornelius and William, respectively, are the most shamelessly ostentatious of the bunch. The Vanderbilts fancied themselves American royalty, which explains the gilt and marble everywhere. Rosecliff was a popular Gilded Age party spot, with its 80-by-40-foot ballroom topped with a trompe l'ocil sky ceiling. This Versailles-inspired mansion is the one that shows up in the movies *True Lies* and *The Great Gatsby*. Kingscote is the most charming, and Chateau-sur-Mer has the most Victorian froufrou. I'm partial to Beechwood: The summer home of society queen Mrs. Astor is — compared with its neighbors — modest, and the tours here are conducted by actors playing the roles of Mrs. Astor's friends, relatives, and servants.

While you're on Bellevue Avenue, leave time for a

An Old-Fashioned Movie Theater

Paula Bodah, managing editor of *Rhode Island Monthly*, says that the Jane Pickens Theater in Newport is "one of the ten things Rhode Islanders are glad we saved." It is one of those nice old theaters with a big velvet curtain and a balcony. The movies here are occasional first-runs, art and foreign films, and the artsier of the Hollywood films (like Merchant-Ivory British period pieces). You've got to hand it to owner Joe Jarvis; he just won't quit. Jarvis has been faced with the prospect of closing the doors more than once. In April 1992, it actually happened. But two months later, with the support of friends and community volunteers, Joe Jarvis reopened the splendid old Washington Square theater. Movie lovers in Newport will be forever grateful.

Jane Pickens Theater, 49 Touro St., Newport. 401-846-5252.

shopping trip along the Travers Block, a long set of Victorian brick-and-shingle-style storefronts. The William Vareika Fine Arts Gallery (on the adjacent Casino Block) displays splendid paintings by American artists of the 18th, 19th, and early 20th centuries, including many who lived in and painted Newport. For a lunchtime respite, head to La Forge Casino Restaurant for a lobster salad roll and iced cappuccino. Ask to sit in the courtyard overlooking the International Tennis Hall of Fame, where the only professional grass-court tournament in the country is played.

Newport's history of religious tolerance is reflected in its many houses of worship: The Friends Meeting House, 1699, is the oldest religious structure in New England; the Seventh Day Baptist Meeting House, circa 1729, is the oldest Sabbatarian meetinghouse in the country; and Touro Synagogue, 1759, is the oldest synagogue in North America. The Channing Memorial Church and the Newport Congregational Church have stained-glass windows by the 19th-century artist John La Farge, an on-and-off resident of Newport. Trinity Church has a pipe organ that was tested by George Frideric Handel before it was shipped from England. St. Mary's Church houses Rhode Island's oldest Roman Catholic parish and was the site of the 1953 wedding of Jacqueline Bouvier and John Fitzgerald Kennedy.

If you tire of history and houses, retreat to a restaurant. The Black Pearl attracts the yachting crowd, who come to be seen as much as to enjoy the clam chowder. The Place at Yesterday's serves the most exciting food in town; what they can do with red snapper! My favorite is the White Horse Tavern, the oldest tavern in the country, for its true Colonial feel and excellent continental fare.

Although you might not decide then and there to live in Newport, I guarantee you'll dream of it.

– Paula M. Bodah

Editors' Picks for Newport

General Information

The Newport County Convention and Visitors' Bureau and the Visitor Information Center, 23 America's Cup Ave., Newport, RI 02840. 800-976-5122, 401-845-9123. (Its office is a good spot to park your car.) (www.gonewport.com)

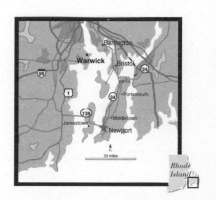

Where to Stay

Newport has literally dozens of bed-and-breakfast establishments. Contact **Bed and Breakfast of Newport,** 33 Russell Ave., Newport, RI 02840. 800-800-8765, 401-846-5408. (www.bbnewport.com)

Or contact **Bed and Breakfast of Rhode Island,** P.O. Box 3291, Newport, RI 02840. 800-828-0000, 401-849-1298. (www.visitnewport.com/bedandbreakfast)

Here are a few we've visited:

Ivy Lodge, 12 Clay St. (one block off Bellevue Ave.), Newport, RI 02840. 800-834-6865, 401-849-6865. A rambling Stanford White-designed 1886 house. Right in the mansion district and a half mile from the Cliff Walk, this big-porched Victorian has eight guest rooms (all with private baths) done in antiques and chintz. Open year-round. Breakfast included. $135-$185.

The Villa Liberté, 22 Liberty St., Newport, RI 02840. 800-392-3717, 401-846-7444. Classy contemporary rooms with plenty of space, a short walk from the center of activity. This completely redone inn with 12 guest rooms in the main house and three apartment suites in a separate house has a colorful, if shady (once a brothel) past, but ask about it. Open year-round. Breakfast included. $89-$145, suites $129-$225. (www.villaliberte.com)

Admiral Benbow Inn, 93 Pelham Street, Newport, RI 02840. 800-343-2863, 401-848-8000. An 1855 Italianate Victorian, located on a historic hill within walking distance of many Newport attractions. The 15 guest rooms with private baths are furnished with period antiques, and some have large Palladian windows with harbor views. Open year-round. Continental breakfast included. $65-$170. (www.admiralsinns.com)

The Inn at Shadow Lawn, 120 Miantonomi Ave., Newport/Middletown, RI 02842. 800-352-3750, 401-847-0902. An 1856 Italianate-style mansion on two acres, formerly home to Hamilton Hoppin. Features include stained glass, parquet floors, elephant-skin wallpaper (yes, it's true!), and fireplaces, all nicely restored. There are eight large guest rooms, all with private baths, refrigerators, fireplaces, cable TV, VCRs, and air-conditioning; complimentary bottle of wine. Open year-round. Full breakfast included. $55-$155. (www.shadowlawn.com)

Where to Eat

The Black Pearl, Bannister's Wharf, Newport. 401-846-5264. The Black Pearl attracts the yachting crowd, who come to be seen as much as to enjoy the clam chowder. The former boathouse and sail loft now houses two dining options: the Commodore's Room, where the prices are as haute as the cuisine, and the more informal tavern section, where you can have something as simple as a burger and crock of clam chowder or as substantial as a swordfish dinner. Open daily nearly year-round, closed month of January. The tavern open for lunch and dinner; $$-$$$. The Commodore's Room dinner only; $$$-$$$$.

La Forge Casino Restaurant, 186 Bellevue Ave., Newport. 401-847-0418. For a lunchtime respite, head to La Forge for a lobster salad roll and iced cappuccino. Ask to sit in the courtyard overlooking the International Tennis Hall of Fame, where the only professional grass-court tournament in the country is played. Open year-round daily for lunch and dinner, except Thanksgiving and Christmas. $$-$$$.

The Rhumb Line, 62 Bridge St., Newport. 401-849-6950. Set in the Point neighborhood, a Colonial settlement just a little removed from the bustle of downtown Newport, the Rhumb Line for years has served as a getaway place for both natives and tourists "in the know." The menu is straightforward, and you can't go wrong with either the seafood or meat dishes. Mussels marinière and a vegetarian wild-rice fajita are favorite appetizers with habitués, and any one of the veal or seafood entrées makes an excellent second course. Open year-round Wednesday-Sunday for lunch; call ahead for dinner. $$.

Scales and Shells, 527 Thames St., Newport. 401-846-3474. Two excellent dining choices here, both open year-round. Open daily for dinner; $$-$$$. And for arguably the best seafood dinner in Newport, reserve a table in the new formal upstairs dining room of Scales and Shells, called Upscales. Open daily at 6 P.M.; $$$-$$$$.

The White Horse Tavern, corner Farewell and Marlborough sts., Newport. 401-849-3600. First licensed as a tavern in 1687, the venerable White Horse Tavern now serves a sophisticated blend of American and Continental cuisines in a meticulously restored historic landmark. Open year-round Thursday-Sunday for lunch. Open daily for dinner. $$$$.

What to See

Astors' Beechwood, 580 Bellevue Ave., Newport. 401-846-3772. Unlike the other Newport mansions, Beechwood is still "inhabited." A living history tour is offered here, depicting the year 1891 by using actors and actresses (in period costumes) who portray the role of Mrs. Astor's servants, family members, and guests. Open mid-May to late October daily 10-5, occasionally closed early for private events. Mid-November to mid-December, call ahead for hours and prices. $8.75, seniors $6.75, students 14 and over $7.25, children 6-13 $6.75, under 6 free. A family package available for $25 (two adults and two or more children).

The Preservation Society of Newport County, 424 Bellevue Ave., Newport. 401-847-1000. Under the auspices of the Preservation Society of Newport County, nine properties, six of which are mansions of the very rich and famous, are open to the public. The Breakers, built by Cornelius Vanderbilt II, covers one acre, contains 70 rooms, has running hot and cold freshwater and saltwater bathroom taps. If ostentation is your thing, this is the place. Chateau-sur-Mer is one of Newport's older mansions and has the most Victorian froufrou. The Elms, although perhaps the best furnished of the mansions, is well known for its gardens. Kingscote is a modest mansion — compared with the others. Marble House, built in 1892, retains its original sumptuous furnishings. Rosecliff was a popular Gilded Age party spot, with its 80-by-40-foot ballroom topped with a trompe l'oeil sky ceiling. For the Newport mansions, allow at least an hour for each, but limit yourself: All that glitters this much can become tiring in one day. Open daily 10-5. The Breakers: $10, students $6, children 6-11 $4. All other mansions: $8, students $5, children 6-11 $3.50. Combination tickets available. (www.newportmansions.org)

Hammersmith Farm, Ocean Dr., Newport. 401-846-7346. Long before Jackie became O, she was Bouvier and spent summers here. When she was Kennedy, this was the summer

White House. Tour the house with original furnishings and enjoy the extensive gardens designed by Frederick Law Olmsted. Open April-November daily 10-5. $8.50, children 6-12 $3.50, under 6 free.

International Tennis Hall of Fame and Tennis Museum, 194 Bellevue Ave., Newport. 401-849-3990. A building called the Casino houses this must-see museum for anyone who has ever lobbed a tennis ball or been glued to the television during Wimbledon. Open year-round daily 9:30-5. $8, seniors and students $6, children 6-16 $4, under 6 free. (www.tennisfame.org)

Cliff Walk, Newport. The sea and mansions line this 3½-mile walk along high cliffs, providing the best views of both. Start at Memorial Boulevard at Easton's Beach, and if you go all the way, you'll stop at Ledge Road near the end of Bellevue Ave. Open daily 9-9.

Touro Synagogue, 85 Touro St., Newport. 401-847-4794. Jewish settlers were among the earliest in town, and the congregation hired one of the most promising architects, Peter Harrison, to design its synagogue in 1763. It's the oldest synagogue in the United States and is considered by many to be one of the finest examples of 18th-century Georgian architecture in America. Tours are given every half hour when synagogue is open; last tour begins a half hour before closing. Open Memorial Day-July 4 and Labor Day-Columbus Day: tours Monday-Friday 1-3 P.M., Sunday 11-3. July 4-Labor Day: tours Sunday-Friday 10-5. Columbus Day-Memorial Day: tours Sunday 1-3 P.M., Monday-Friday 2 P.M. (one tour only). No tours on Saturday or Jewish holidays. Admission charge for groups only (call ahead to make arrangements for group tour). Individuals and families need not call ahead. (www.nps.gov/tosy)

Our Towns

Marlow, New Hampshire. *(photo by Arthur Boufford, courtesy New Hampshire Tourism)*

Our Towns

A Sampler of
New England's Prettiest

FOR AS LONG AS I'VE BEEN DRIVING AROUND NEW England, I've never run out of towns that look just like their postcards. A white-steepled church fronts the town green, which is bordered by black-shuttered white clapboard houses; or squat Capes clad in weather-beaten shingles match the shacks where the lobstermen work down by the harbor.

Sometimes a friend steers me toward one of these towns. More often I'm lost, and the town is the reward for driving in circles or down endless two-lane roads.

Everyone's definition of a pretty town probably differs, but I look for a sense of time passed by, a preservation of the past, and a very real present. Qualifying towns don't have to lie far off the beaten path; they may be under your nose. And there should be somewhere to eat. I'm not being romantic when I say I've discovered most of these places when lost. I've usually been quite lost — and quite hungry.

Here, then, is a highly subjective list of my contenders for the prettiest towns in New England.

Kittery Point, Maine

If you think that Kittery is just the mall-to-mall strip of outlets along Route 1, you have a very pleasant surprise waiting. Make a detour on Route 103 toward Kittery Point, the oldest town in Maine, first settled in 1623.

The road rolls along to the sea, passing through sparsely populated countryside. Where there's a sharp turn, look closely for the grand (and private) Lady Pepperrell House, built in 1760. Across the street is the First Congregational Church, built in 1730.

Farther along, the Fort McClary Memorial is the remnants of a fort named for a local soldier who died at the Battle of Bunker Hill. A cluster of houses, a post office, a church, and a market describe the town. The market is Frisbee's, which claims, at 170 years, to be the oldest family-owned grocery store in North America. On the right you won't miss the sign for Cap'n Simeon's Galley, a restaurant overlooking Portsmouth harbor that serves a very good lobster roll and grilled fish amid a relentless nautical decor.

But if you want lobster outdoors in the Maine tradition, continue on Pepperrell Road and look for the sign for Chauncey Creek Lobster Pier, which will direct you down narrow Chauncey Creek Road. On your right is the Lobster Pier. With a view of forested Gerrish Island from one of the brightly painted picnic tables on the deck and perhaps a cooling breeze coming upstream, this feels miles from anywhere. The Lobster Pier serves lobster — the lobster rolls

Approaching the Lady Pepperrell House in historic Kittery Point.
(*photo by Stephen O. Muskie*)

come doused with paprika on an untoasted bun — clams, and steamed mussels in wine and garlic. You have to bring your own wine or beer.

After lunch, take the turn onto Gerrish Island and visit Fort Foster. I'm no great fan of fortifications, but this one has a view of the distant Isles of Shoals (the far lighthouse is on White Island; the closer one is Whaleback Light at the mouth of the Piscataqua River) and rocky coast to clamber.

***

Cap'n Simeon's Galley, 90 Pepperrell Rd. (Rte. 103), Kittery Point. 207-439-3655. Open in summer daily for lunch and dinner; off-season closed Tuesday. $-$$.

Chauncey Creek Lobster Pier, Chauncey Creek Rd., Kittery Point. 207-439-1030. Most entrées are served à la carte, and the lobster is priced daily. Chicken and pizza are offered for those non-lobster lovers. Open Mother's Day-Columbus Day daily for lunch and dinner; closed Monday in September; open weekends in October. $.

Kingfield, Maine

Most people make the trek to Kingfield, in Maine's western mountains, to go skiing at its big neighbor, Sugarloaf/USA. I can think of at least two other good reasons to visit.

Named for William King, its founder and Maine's first governor, Kingfield has matured on the ski business, but it was born on lumber mills. Main Street looks as if it would be comfortable in the Old West, its clapboard stores bellying up to the road. The Herbert Hotel, a Victorian whimsy built in 1918, has been restored with a Gilded Age feeling and acts as command center in town. For dinner, cognoscenti move to One Stanley Avenue, which prides itself on using fresh, local ingredients. It is known as one of the best restaurants in the state.

Kingfield has a favorite son, actually two of them. The twin Stanley brothers, of Stanley Steamer automobile fame, were born here. The Stanley Museum, in a former school-

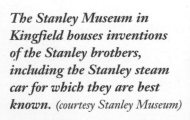

The Stanley Museum in Kingfield houses inventions of the Stanley brothers, including the Stanley steam car for which they are best known. (courtesy Stanley Museum)

house, teaches just enough about them through explanatory panels and exhibits — two restored and running Stanley Steamer motor cars, letters, some technical knickknacks — to make you realize what an amazing invention an automobile is. Look for the letter from the widow of F. E. Stanley, who died in a car accident in 1918, a most poignant description of love lost.

But the unexpected delight is the display of photographs by Chansonetta Stanley, the brothers' beautifully named and very talented sister. Long before most women had careers — or were photographers — Chansonetta captured in black-and-white photos the rural world of Kingfield (and beyond). The faces of those farm girls pictured 100 years ago look as fresh as any teenager's today. For all of Kingfield's Victorian charm, its 20th-century ski aura, and its famous Stanley brothers, it's Chansonetta's story that stays with me on the long drive home.

~~~

The Herbert Hotel, Main St. (jct. rtes. 16 and 27N), P.O. Box 67, Kingfield, ME 04947. 800-843-4372, 207-265-2000. Twenty-eight rooms, all with private baths and some with Jacuzzi tubs. Open year-round. Continental breakfast included. $59-$98. Open Thursday-Sunday for dinner. Reservations recommended. $$-$$$. (www.byme.com/theherbert)

One Stanley Avenue, 1 Stanley Ave., Kingfield. 207-265-5541. Classic cuisine, considered one of the best restaurants in the area. Choice of two dining rooms. Open mid-April to December Tuesday-Sunday for dinner. Reservations recommended. $$-$$$.

Stanley Museum, School St., Kingfield. 207-265-2729. Open year-round Tuesday-Sunday 1-4 P.M., closed weekends November-April. $2, under 12 $1.

New Harbor, Maine

At the eastern side of Pemaquid Point, this town has had about as picture-perfect a harbor as one could wish for — for centuries. This was the home of Samoset, the Indian who startled the Pilgrims in Plymouth in 1621 by greeting them with, "Much welcome, Englishmen." Seems Samoset had hobnobbed with the English sailors who fished off nearby Monhegan Island.

Today New Harbor is small and sheltered, ringed with pine trees and home to as many working lobster boats as sailing boats. Best of all, you can have a nice seat from which to view all this lovely scenery at Shaw's Fish and Lobster Wharf Restaurant. Order your lobster and iced tea, then pick your picnic table out on the deck. Fishermen unload their catch, and the boat to Monhegan Island takes off from here as well. With so much to see, you'd better order a strawberry short-

New Harbor on the eastern side of Pemaquid Point is one of Maine's most picturesque working harbors.
(photo by Stephen O. Muskie)

cake to keep up your energy.

A trip to the very tip of the peninsula will take you to the 1827 Pemaquid Light and its tiny Fisherman's Museum. Here the earth rolls into the sea with big, wave-smoothed rocks, perfect for scrambling over in late-afternoon light.

~~~

Fishermen's Museum, at Pemaquid Point on Rte. 130, New Harbor. 207-677-2494. Open Memorial Day to mid-October Monday-Saturday 10-5, Sunday 11-5. Donation.

Shaw's Fish and Lobster Wharf Restaurant, Rte. 32, New Harbor. 207-677-2200. Open late May to mid-October daily 11-9. $-$$.

Grafton, Vermont

The approach is on a washboard dirt road, the perfect entrance to this secluded slice of Greek Revival New England in the Vermont mountains. This, you think, is how our ancestors traveled, being bounced about by bumps. Protected from macadam, Grafton is a gem of the early 1800s. True, it's had a little help in looking so pristine and all from the wealthy Windham Foundation, which bought and restored the entire town. But there's no denying it's pretty.

Everyone's first reaction to Grafton is to wander up and down the streets. Everyone's second reaction to Grafton is to take up residence in one of the rocking chairs that line the porch of the Old Tavern, which has been offering rooms to the weary since 1801. I'm sure that for at least that long, carloads of New Yorkers have been transformed into rocking hayseeds by this porch.

The Old Tavern offers a small-town experience with a stay in one of the inn's rooms, in one of its cottages, or in one of the seven guest houses tucked around town. You'll be in

The porch of the Old Tavern proves irresistible to visitors and sheep — Grafton is home to one of the state's largest flocks. (courtesy the Old Tavern at Grafton)

good company — among visitors have been Ulysses S. Grant, Teddy Roosevelt, Henry David Thoreau, and Rudyard Kipling. For the active, there are 30 kilometers of hiking, tennis courts, and a natural swimming pond — but those rocking chairs are tempting.

All that rocking and watching nothing in particular works up an appetite. The inn has a pretty greenhouse setting for its lunch guests, housed in the rustically renovated barn and furnished with a herd of Windsor chairs. The only other hub of action in town is the General Store, which stocks Vermont goods as well as the local Grafton Cheese Company cheddar, the basis for any successful picnic. Which, I suppose, you could have in a rocking chair, if you really wanted.

⌒⌒

The Old Tavern at Grafton, Rte. 35, Grafton, VT 05146. 800-843-1801, 802-843-2231. Offers 65 rooms divided between the inn and 11 houses. Some are located throughout the village, while others are secreted away in the surrounding woods. Full country breakfast included. $125-$195. Open Memorial Day-late October daily for lunch and dinner; open weekends all year for lunch; closed April. Reservations recommended. $$$-$$$$. (www.old-tavern.com)

Hancock, New Hampshire

In the brilliance of autumn, half the world is climbing Mount Monadnock and the other half is visiting nearby Hancock. Established in 1779, the town was named for John Hancock, who owned a lot of it but neither visited nor, according to the weighty *History of Hancock*, "appeared to have in the least interested himself in its welfare." Despite that, Hancock (the town) turned into a charming village with a pretty Victorian bandstand, handsome houses set back modestly from the street, and a Congregational church that dates to 1820, its bell cast in Paul Revere's foundry two years after his death. Stroll the

Opened in 1789, the Hancock Inn is the state's oldest continually operated inn and one of many historic buildings in town. (courtesy New Hampshire Tourism)

main street, have lunch at the new gourmet deli, Fiddle-heads, and check into the Hancock Inn for dinner and a good night's sleep (as travelers have been doing at this inn for more than 200 years).

Hancock Inn, Main St., P.O. Box 96, Hancock, NH 03449. 800-525-1789, 603-525-3318. Despite's its strong claim for being the oldest inn in the state, later renovations give it a distinctly 19th-century feel. All guest rooms (11 rooms, four suites) have private baths, some have canopy beds. Open year-round. Full breakfast included. $106-$172, suites $192-$210. Open nightly (except Christmas night) for dinner. Reservations recommended. $$-$$$. (www.hancockinn.com)

Harrisville, New Hampshire

New Hampshire

★Harrisville

From Hancock take Route 137 south, and in a little over three miles look for Hancock Road on your right. This will take you past Lake Skatutakee and into the tiny town of Har-risville. This is perhaps my favorite of all. Here tidy brick buildings and a large granite mill are strung along the millstream that once powered a woolen mill. On the hill sits a long boardinghouse. The buildings are fully restored, thanks to a nonprofit group that leases them out to various businesses, including the interna-tionally known Harrisville Designs, makers of looms and yarns for handweavers and knitters. If you turn right at Har-risville Designs and cross the bridge, you'll find a group of five millworkers' houses called "Peanut Row." Beyond these is Sunset Beach, the town's private little beach and a nice spot for a picnic. Harrisville is the village most painted by artists (even more than Hancock) and is one of the oldest existing textile communities in the country, a National Historic Landmark village.

There is hardly a lovelier sight than the Harrisville Public Library reflected in the canal of this classic New Hampshire mill village.
(photo by Arthur Boufford, courtesy New Hampshire Tourism)

Harrisville Designs Weaving Center, P.O. Box 806, Harrisville. 603-827-3996. Weekend and multiday weaving workshops are held throughout the year. Request a schedule. Store open Tuesday-Saturday 10-5.

Sugar Hill, New Hampshire

This is Sugar Hill: a bend on Route 117, a curve, and a hill. A beautiful spread of barn and fields called Iris Farm that's best seen in morning mists, a small inn called Hilltop Inn, and a restaurant devoted to flapjacks called Polly's Pancake Parlor. It doesn't sound like much, but trust me, it is.

Hilltop Inn, Main St., Sugar Hill, NH 03585. 800-770-5695, 603-823-5695. Six rooms with private baths, antiques, and generous breakfasts. $80-$175. (www.hilltopinn.com)

Polly's Pancake Parlor, Rte. 117, Sugar Hill. 603-823-5575. Open Mother's Day to mid-October Monday-Friday 7-3, Saturday-Sunday 7-7. $.

The Hilltop Inn in Sugar Hill is an 1895 Victorian set in the White Mountains, just north of Franconia Notch. (courtesy Hilltop Inn)

Old Deerfield, Massachusetts

Time and Route 5 may have passed Old Deerfield by, but history lovers do not. Along this historic town's wide mile-long Main Street, a dozen of the houses are preserved as museums. At first glance, it's not easy to tell which are house museums and which are private homes — all are immaculately restored and maintained. Twice sacked by Indian raids, Old Deerfield is preserved from modernity's raid by Historic Deerfield, which runs many of the house museums. The fascinating (and compact) Memorial Hall Museum is run by the Pocumtuck Valley Memorial Association.

In a town first settled in the 1660s, there's lots of history to absorb. Some of the museums feature the architecture of the house, others emphasize a particular collection such as silver or textiles. While Deerfield focuses on its history, it does so without the costumed guides of Plimoth Plantation or Old Sturbridge Village. A walk down Main Street takes you past houses built in the 1700s, with their dark facades, and Deerfield Academy, with its flurry of prep-school students. A walk in autumn surrounded by yellow leaves is especially pleasant.

If the number and scope of the houses is a little daunting to you (or you have a car of fidgety kids), at least visit the Memorial Hall Museum, which sums up tidily the town's history through photographs, paintings, and historic costumes. Most celebrated in its collection is the doorway of the John Sheldon House, which was razed in the mid-19th century. The door, however, warranted saving because it had survived the February 1704 Indian attack — hatchet marks and poundings are still evident, still capable of sending shivers down your spine. It's all housed in a stolid brick building, built in 1798 for Deerfield Academy.

~⌒⌒⌐

Historic Deerfield, Old Deerfield. 413-774-5581.

You won't find a prettier stroll than Main Street in Old Deerfield, Massachusetts. (*photo by Amanda Merullo, courtesy Historic Deerfield, Inc.*)

Open daily 9:30-4:30. Admission to all historic houses $12, children 6-21 $6. Tickets good for two consecutive days. (www.historic-deerfield.org)

Memorial Hall Museum, Memorial St., Old Deerfield. 413-774-3768. Open May-October daily 9:30-4:30. $6, children $3, under 6 free. (www.old-deerfield.org)

Marblehead, Massachusetts

Route 114 is a sadist's idea of a road. Yes, there are signs for its twists and bends, but they're hidden behind overgrown branches. But the payoff is well worth the frustration.

For beautiful coastal settings, Marblehead is hard to beat. Downtown, settled in 1629 and known appropriately as Old Town, seems to tumble to the long harbor, which is filled with fancy yachts and ringed with lush estates and yacht clubs. If you don't own a boat or have a close friend

Marblehead's houses perch above its snug fishing harbor. (photo by Dennis P. Curtin)

who does, the next best view of the harbor is from
Crocker Park.

Settled by fishermen from West England and the
Channel Islands, Marblehead by 1649 was called "the greatest Towne for fishing in New England." By 1720 its
shipowners had expanded beyond fishing into overseas trading. The oldest houses, jumbled together with minuscule
gardens by the harbor, reflect the settlers' humble origins
and miserly desire to save timber and preserve heat; the
houses of the later shippers display 18th-century conspicu-
ous consumption.

The layout of Marblehead follows the perverse logic of
any early seaside village. Streets twist and end abruptly as
they skirt the hills and rolling topography. Getting lost here
— on your way to find Front Street and the harbor — is the
point of going to Marblehead. Unfortunately many visitors
get no farther than the boutiques along Washington Street,
which is a shame. To help you wander, stop by the chamber
of commerce's information booth for a booklet with a walking tour of town.

At some point you need to make your way to Abbot
Hall to see the celebrated painting *The Spirit of '76*, located in the selectmen's room. Make lunch a picnic in
Crocker Park, or a eat a waterside meal of fish-and-chips
at the Barnacle.

~

Marblehead Chamber of Commerce, 62 Pleasant St.,
P.O. Box 76, Marblehead, MA 01945. 781-631-2868. Stop
in at the information booth at the corner of Pleasant and
Essex streets for a booklet with a self-guided walking tour of
downtown. Open during summer weekdays noon-6, weekends 10-6; off-season open weekends only, hours vary.
(www.marbleheadchamber.org)

The Barnacle, 141 Front St., Marblehead. 781-631-4236. A
small, homey restaurant right on the water that just happens

to serve the best fish-and-chips in town. Open daily for lunch and dinner; closed Tuesday and January-March. $$.

Trattoria Il Panino, 126 Washington St., Marblehead. 781-631-3900. This gracious restaurant located in the heart of historic Marblehead specializes in Tuscan Mediterranean cuisine. It features an eclectic and very popular wine cellar bar and al fresco dining during the summer in its outdoor courtyard. Open nightly for dinner. Reservations recommended. $$-$$$.

Brewster, Massachusetts

 When I begin to think that Cape Cod is all built up and way too popular, I drive Route 6A, skirting the northern rim, to be reminded that Cape Cod still has its charms. The towns along the way — Sandwich, Barnstable, Yarmouthport — all have handsome houses built by sea captains and town centers humming with antiques stores and markets. They also have, for some reason, an incredible number of bird carvers nesting here.

Brewster is not the oldest; settled in 1656, it's younger than Sandwich, the first town settled on the Cape in 1637. But it's my favorite for dining. It may be difficult to get reservations for dinner at Chillingsworth, but it tops the Cape's list of restaurants every year.

Antiquing along Main Street caters to both the serious collector and the seeker of collectibles. Two churches and an ancient graveyard complete the town.

In early spring the herring make a frenzied show at the Stony Brook Mill on Stony Brook Road. Year-round the Cape Cod Museum of Natural History introduces children and grown-ups to nature's side of the Cape — there are aquariums of amphibians, displays of shells and bugs, depictions of the havoc that pollution is wreaking. Check the tide schedule, then follow one of the paths behind the museum that leads out to the marshes.

With all this activity, you'd think Brewster would be my choice for a busy weekend. Not so. I like Brewster best for curling up with a book for the day at my inn.

~~~⌐

Cape Cod Museum of Natural History, Rte. 6A, P.O. Box 1710, Brewster. 508-896-3867. Open year-round Monday-Saturday 9:30-4:30, Sunday 11-4:30. $5, seniors $4.50, children 5-12 $2, under 5 free. (www.ccmnh.com)

Chillingsworth, 2449 Main St. (Rte. 6A), Brewster. 508-896-3640. Open Tuesday-Sunday for lunch and dinner. $$-$$$$.

Old Sea Pines Inn, 2553 Main St. (Rte. 6A), P.O. Box 1070, Brewster. 508-896-6114. The inn offers 23 rooms, 18 with private baths. $55-$150. (www.oldseapinesinn.com)

Old Wethersfield, Connecticut

When architects see something they like, they tend to stand in one place and waggle their hands a lot. Strange words like *dentil, quoin, pilaster,* and *oriel* spring from their lips. If you'd like a demonstration of this, take an architect to Old Wethersfield, just south of Hartford. Established in 1634, this town was an important port on the Connecticut River — until the river changed its course and left Old Wethersfield behind. Passed by, the town retained its past — and grew as a suburb of Hartford. Today it is an unusual community because it has at least one house in every architectural style from every period in America, from an early Colonial with overhang to low-slung ranch houses and everything in between. Architects go wild.

Wethersfield grew on agriculture, primarily onions. There are a number of historic buildings open to the public, including the Webb-Deane-Stevens Museum, a melding of three 18th-century houses. Inside you can see the contrasting lifestyles of the resident diplomat, merchant, and leather worker. George Washington really did sleep in the Webb house. Gardeners, here also is the home of Comstock, Ferre & Co., the nation's oldest continuously operating seed company.

After cruising around the streets of town, drive to the old cove, what was the original bustling harbor, to view Wethersfield's — and the country's — only remaining 17th-century warehouse. This now-quiet spot saw exports of fish and salt beef in the 1640s and imports of rum, molasses, and wool in the 1700s. All the commotion of busy trade seems very far away, especially when you're standing under a tree listening to birdsong.

$\sim$

The Standish House, 222 Main St., Old Wethersfield. 860-257-1151. Excellent continental cuisine, offering 15 different appetizers and soups, over 20 entrées, including the all-time favorite filet mignon of beef with exotic mushroom

These beautiful 18th-century houses are a part of the Webb-Deane-Stevens Museum in Old Wethersfield, Connecticut. (courtesy Webb-Deane-Stevens Museum)

ragout. Open daily for dinner. $$$.

Webb-Deane-Stevens Museum, 211 Main St., Old Wethersfield. 860-529-0612. Open May 1-October 31, Wednesday-Monday 10-4. $8, children 6-11 $4, under 6 free.

Little Compton, Rhode Island

Rhode Islanders quickly name Little Compton as the prettiest town in their state, but they won't tell you how to get there. This small town, down in the Sakonnet area, is not a wide spot in the road — it's a bend in the road, twisting itself around its formidable white church. This is just a warning: If you head down to Sakonnet in search of Little Compton, you should expect to get lost. The locals around this easternmost strip of Rhode Island take a perverse pleasure in not putting up road signs where they're most needed, like at intersections and forks in the road.

It's easier to get to Tiverton Four Corners, which is, if you know the way, pretty close to Little Compton. Those who make it to Tiverton Four Corners — literally just a crossroads — can stop at the gourmet's mecca, Provender, for a take-home loaf of freshly baked bread. And some directions. Then set out across the undulating farm fields for Little Compton. The houses get closer together, there's the playing field, then the graveyard, and you can't miss the church.

The reward at Little Compton is the Commons, a diner next to Wilbur's store, an emporium of this and that and some more this. When you arrive in Little Compton, perch on a stool along the counter of the Commons and have a plate of jonnycakes, any time of day. But lunch is just as regional. Chowder comes in a sturdy porcelain cup, clam fritters are big and crunchy, and an order of vanilla ice cream would be enough to satisfy two parties with a sweet tooth each. All is best eaten on the shaded patio on a steamy summer afternoon. Here you can watch the world of Little Compton go by — a pickup truck, a pair of ladies heading for the Grange hall, the neighbors who check the notices tacked up by Wilbur's. Maybe a dog will trot by.

Provender, 3883 Main Rd., Tiverton. 401-624-8096. This gourmet food deli is known for its literary eating habits. Choose from the popular Scarlet Letter sandwich (turkey with tarragon mayo, alfalfa sprouts and cranberry sauce), the Brideshead Revisited (roast beef, horseradish mayo, cheddar cheese, and lettuce), or the Dr. Bombay (curried chicken salad with mango chutney and lettuce) on any of a dozen varieties of bread baked daily. Open in summer daily 9-5; in winter Tuesday-Sunday 9-5. $.

The Commons, Little Compton. 401-635-4388. If you're not in the mood for jonnycakes, try the seafood pie or a lobster roll. Open daily for breakfast, lunch, and dinner. $.

– Janice Brand